MY 50 YEARS

BUDDHIST PRACTICE

Dealing with Depression,

Serious Illness &

Everyday Life

By

Michael Lisagor

Published by Beabuddha Press

Copyright 2021 by Michael Lisagor

All rights reserved

Printed in the United States of America

10 9 8 7 6 5 4 3 2 1

Library of Congress Cataloging-in-Publication Data

My Fifty Years of Buddhist Practice

ISBN: 9798612841876

Nonfiction > Religion > Buddhism

Nonfiction > Self-Help > Personal Growth

TABLE OF CONTENTS

Prologue 7
Growing Older is a Laughing Matter 9
Can We Really Make a Difference? 12
Mastering My Mind 14
Is there Life after Life? 17
A Buddhist & a Christian Meet in a Taxi 20
Finding Old Ways to Communicate 23
Be the Change 26
Rewriting My Story 28
Helping Students Worry Less 31
Overcoming Ourselves to Help Others 34
Creating Hope in Difficult Times 37
Dear Depressed 42
Overcoming My Fear 44
Changing Mental & Karmic Constructs 48
Cells that Fire Together Wire Together 50
A Great Path to Peace 52
A Buddhist & Therapist Find Self-Love 55
When Teenage Angst is Not Just a Phase 58
Moving Past Despair and Blame 62
Feeling the Social Media Blues 65
Fifty Years But Who's Counting 68
Being the Father I Never Had 73

Getting Comfortable with Discomfort 75
I'm a Buddha, You're a Buddha, Too 77
It's Never Too Late 80
Enlightened Fatherhood 82
I Was Never Happy Being Depressed 90
The Space Between Birth and Death 92
The Pain is Mainly in My Brain 98
Are You Too Busy to Say No? 101
Stepping Through the Ten Worlds 104
Discovering My True Worth 109
Learning from My Mistakes 112
Relieving Suffering Isn't Optional 114
When Good Enough is Good Enough 117
Each Child is Our Responsibility 119
Tricking Your Mind, Not Your Karma 121
When Past, Present & Future Collide 124
I Won't Be Afraid 126
Rub-a-dub-dub, Too Much in My Tub! 129
What is True Happiness? 132
For Further Information 144
Glossary of Buddhist Terms 145

Daisaku Ikeda has said, "Words spoken from the heart have the power to change a person's life. They can even melt the icy walls of mistrust that separate peoples and nations."

Václav Havel in his essay, "Orientation of the Heart," describes hope as "a state of mind, not a state of the world."

Prologue

My 50 Years of Buddhist Practice: Dealing with Depression, Serious Illness & Everyday Life is about the lessons I have learned from my daily practice of SGI Nichiren Buddhism. These 41 articles and talks, written between 2016 and 2019, reflect a period of me looking backward with intense self-reflection which resulted in the successful resolution of many years of hurt and sadness.

The book describes how Buddhism, with its teachings of personal and social transformation, and psychotherapy have helped my wife and me deal with chronic illness, childhood trauma, depression, parenting, aging and creating hope in this challenging world.

This is a sequel to *Romancing the Buddha* (third edition available on amazon.com) which was also a successful one-man show that can be viewed on YouTube.

As stand-alone chapters that can be read in any order, there is some minor duplication of overall themes and explanations for the sake of clarity. The views expressed are solely my own. I have tried to avoid using words to describe my childhood that might trigger certain readers.

While I'm writing this preface, it is lightly raining where we live on an island in the Pacific Northwest. The COVID-19 pandemic is surging for the third time this year. I feel a deep sorrow for the pain and loss being experienced by so many.

My mentor, Daisaku Ikeda, has said, "What our society today needs more than anything is the spirit of empathy – the ability to put ourselves in the shoes of those who are facing hardship and suffering, to understand and share what they are going through. When the spirit of compassion becomes the bedrock of society, and is embodied by society's leaders, the future will be bright with hope."

It is my sincere desire that this book will give this kind of hope and encouragement to whoever reads it!

Sincerely,

Mike

mike@romancingthebuddha.com

www.romancingthebuddha.com

Growing Older is a Laughing Matter

"You don't stop laughing when you grow old, you grow old when you stop laughing." -- George Bernard Shaw

Buddhism teaches that the four sufferings of birth, aging, sickness and death are an inescapable part of life. The important thing is not to be defeated by them. Thanks to my parents, I've already had a victory over the first one. So that leaves aging, sickness and, inevitably, death.

Lately, I've been reflecting on what it means to be 70 years old and moving closer to the end of this life. As a child and teenager who suffered from severe depression, I was too afraid of the present to expend energy worrying about the future, much less old age. Most of the older people I knew back then seemed full of regret and suffering. It wasn't until I started practicing Buddhism that I got a glimpse of a different way to age - one full of hope and vitality instead of fear and sadness.

Buddhist philosopher and author, Daisaku Ikeda, has said that youthfulness originates from life force. There are young people who are disillusioned and there are elderly people who, no matter how the years pass, sparkle with the glow of youthful inner vitality. Still, I can't ignore the fact that my body has slowed down. Slight injuries now have greater consequences. A hurt lower back that might have kept me in bed for a few days took two years to recover. Through this experience, I also learned that my mental attitude significantly affects my ability to heal. My Buddhist practice gives me the wisdom and strength to influence my mind and, accordingly, to lessen my physical and emotional suffering.

My wife, Most Beautiful One (MBO), has had the same experience with her multiple sclerosis (MS). MS involves an immune-mediated process in which an abnormal response of the body's immune system is directed against the central nervous system which is made up of the brain, spinal cord and optic nerves. MBO's symptoms have included chronic fatigue, numbness and, on several occasions, painful facial nerve flare-ups.

The disturbing reality of MS caught her—the always healthy, independent, in control and seemingly invincible woman—totally by surprise. Since first being diagnosed in 1996, she has used her daily practice of chanting Nam myoho renge kyo to help raise her life condition, improve her ability to manage her symptoms and to more quickly recover from several major relapses – the last one about ten years ago.

With the help of this remarkable practice and a compassionate therapist, I turned what could have been a devastating occurrence into the fuel to make personal changes that had continued to elude me, including being able to face and overcome my childhood sadness and anger.

In Buddhist terms, youth has nothing to do with chronological age. Instead it reflects our ability to consistently maintain a hopeful, flexible and tolerant mind.

Unfortunately, right when I am experiencing love for the whole world, I will encounter someone in person or something in the news that triggers negative feelings. Of course, this "stress" is usually what I need to cause me to continue to evolve into a more enlightened, compassionate person. While not always with open arms, I do welcome these opportunities.

There is a saying that goes: "To a fool, old age is a bitter winter; to a wise person it is a golden time." Without my spiritual practice and the support of a loving family and friends, my winter would be bitter indeed. I'm so grateful that this doesn't have to be the case. And I look forward to laughing well into my nineties!

Can We Really Make a Difference?

Many people are feeling overwhelmed by today's uncertain social and political realities. They feel powerless about their ability to make a difference. I recall experiencing a similar despair in the 1960s. I have vivid memories of the school bell ringing three times to alert us to drop beneath our desks in case of an atomic bomb attack. Coupled with the war in Vietnam, the assassination of respected leaders, and the absence of civil rights for a large segment of our population, there seemed to be little reason to have hope for the future. Still, we found ways to socially and politically engage and to maintain hope.

There has actually never been a time in modern human history without conflict, injustice and suffering. There has also never been a time without compassion, resistance and relief. And the world will always reflect this dichotomy and the resulting tension.

The fact there are over seven billion people in the world can make us feel insignificant. What do we matter and how can we possibly make a difference? But each of us is unique. There is no other person exactly like us in the entire universe! There is no other Mike Lisagor and no other you anywhere else. We each get to create our own story. The only question we need to answer is how can we be our best possible selves?

Daisaku Ikeda has said, "When we change, the world changes. The key to all change is in our inner transformation—a change of our hearts and minds. This is human revolution. We all have the power to change. When we realize this truth, we can bring forth that power anywhere, anytime, and in any situation."

We each have the ability to impact the world in significant ways. After all, if a flapping butterfly wing can cause major changes on the other side of the world, surely our efforts for peace and justice, however seemingly insignificant, can counter the fundamental darkness we have all been experiencing.

I believe that the best course of action is to pursue a path of inner change and to manifest the resulting compassion and wisdom as action toward peace in the world around us. How we engage with each person we come in contact with is important. We can and must make a difference.

Mastering My Mind

My inner transformation (human revolution) has included periodic episodes of sadness. As a child, I dealt with physical and emotional trauma as well as a mental illness by working hard to keep my energy elevated and by trying to make everyone laugh. When that didn't work or I ran out of steam, I hid in a dark depression. None of these defensive mental processes served me well as an adult.

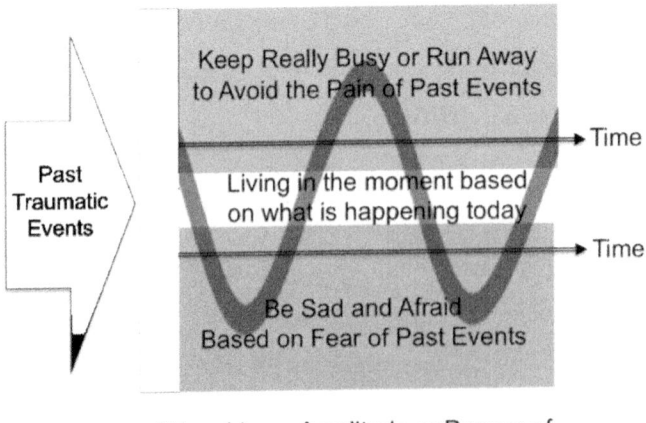

Past Traumatic Events →

Keep Really Busy or Run Away to Avoid the Pain of Past Events → Time

Living in the moment based on what is happening today

Be Sad and Afraid Based on Fear of Past Events → Time

Wavy Line = Amplitude or Degree of Manic &/or Depressive States

The wavy line illustrates how my past coping mechanisms influenced how I perceived and reacted to my present everyday realities even though they are no longer occurring today. That's why one of the objectives of my Buddhist practice and therapy has been to learn how to live in the moment based on what is happening today and not my fears of the future that were based on the past. My years of chanting and therapy have reduced the amplitude of this wavy line.

Another benefit of my Buddhist practice has been the confidence to trust my instincts and inner wisdom. Four years ago, I began to sense a return of some of these destructive mental processes. At the suggestion of my physician, I sought out the help of a psychotherapist who specializes in treating childhood post-traumatic stress with modalities like Eye Movement Desensitization and Reprocessing (EMDR). Working together, I greatly reduced the amplitude of my wavy line!

Nichiren (1222-1282), the founder of Nichiren Buddhism, encouraged us to master our mind instead of allowing our mind to master us. For me, this means being able to observe how I react to various external stimuli such as chronic pain. If I allow myself to embrace a fear of how bad it might get based on past occurrences, it can flare into a painful and extended condition. When this happened recently, I was able to stay in the moment by visualizing this diagram while I was chanting. Observing the pain vanishing in just a few days was very rewarding.

I am now aware of these past thinking patterns and am more readily able to pull myself into the reality of the moment. My goal is to continue to minimize the amplitude of the wavy line so I can live a balanced and emotionally healthy life.

Is there Life after Life?

Most Beautiful One (MBO) and I have had several conversations recently about the nature of life and death and whether our lives are, as Buddhism teaches, eternal. I was inclined to take the eternity of life for granted even though I didn't thoroughly comprehend it. On the other hand, MBO, being of a more sound, skeptical mind, wasn't convinced. So, we began exploring this important concept.

From the perspective of Nichiren Buddhism, our lives in each moment are affected by the karma, the eighth or alaya consciousness; we have formed in previous and current lifetimes. This karma influences the first seven consciousnesses (that's a mouthful!) -- our sight, hearing,

The Nine Consciousnesses
1. Touch
2. Taste
3. Sight
4. Hearing
5. Smell
6. Conscious Mind
7. Subconscious/Limited Egoistic Self
8. Karma store
9. Buddha nature & Nam-myoho-renge-kyo

smell, taste, touch, the integration of this sensory data, and our sense of our individual identity. And this karma is carried over upon our death and influences our experience in between death and birth as well as the circumstances of our next existence. An important question is how we can increase our positive karma. This is why we chant Nam-myoho-renge-kyo, the fundamentally pure consciousness, to bring forth the enlightened nature of a Buddha.

In his book, *Unlocking the Mysteries of Birth & Death*, Daisaku Ikeda discusses Blaise Pascal (1623 -1662), a French thinker and mathematician. Pascal described life after death in terms of probability or wagering theory. Since intelligence hasn't been able to provide definitive proof that there is an afterlife, people who gamble their lives on the chance there is life after death, even if they are wrong, haven't lost anything. On the other hand, if they gamble their life on the chance there isn't an afterlife then, later in life, they will be powerless to alter the course they have taken. Pascal concluded that it makes the most sense to base one's life on the odds that there is life after death.

So, we have concluded that it makes the most sense for us to base our thoughts, actions and deeds on a belief in the eternity of life. In this way, we can appreciate the interconnectedness and interdependence of all things and are motivated to deal with our fellow living beings with compassion and respect. Hopefully, these good causes will positively impact our future existence. I'm wagering they will!

A Buddhist & a Christian Meet in a Taxi

You never know what to expect when you climb into a taxi. My recent Lyft drive from the Boston airport to my grandchildren's home turned into an hour and half traffic crawl. Fortunately, my driver was the talkative type. A native of Guatemala, he and his wife had lived in Boston for eight years.

Our rather mundane conversation shifted to a deeper level when he explained that he hadn't seen his father for several years because he wasn't allowed back into the United States. My driver was afraid he wouldn't be able to return if he left the country to visit him. He mentioned that it was his strong belief in the Bible that had spiritually sustained him. He openly listened as I shared about my Buddhist practice and how it had enabled me and many others to overcome the challenges in our lives. What followed was an informative and refreshing exchange of ideas based on a life-to-life dialogue.

I noticed that whenever we touched upon topics such as gay marriage, he quoted the Bible to explain his opposition. It made me appreciate that Nichiren's letters, written in the 1200s, and Daisaku Ikeda's guidance is encouragement about how to live a better life as opposed to a strict set of behavioral and moral do's and don'ts.

Ikeda has said, "The differences between people need not act as barriers that wound, harm and drive us apart. Rather, these very differences amongst cultures and civilizations should be valued as manifestations of the richness of our shared creativity."

My father, like his father, behaved in a racist manner. Even at a young age, I found his comments to be offensive and embarrassing. I don't think he knew why he believed what he did. Which is ironic, given that his parents had fled Russia to escape persecution for being Jewish.

"Religion is always in danger of growing apart from the people when its leaders forget to reflect carefully on their own behavior and come to look upon themselves as figures of authority." - Daisaku Ikeda

I explained to my driver, that as a Buddhist, I believed that everyone, regardless of race, gender, national origin, color, ethnicity, or religion, has within them a potential enlightened or Buddha nature that they can manifest in this lifetime. So, they are deserving of our respect and compassion. Until humanity embraces this mindset, we are destined to continue a cycle of religious violence.

My remarks caused a definite pause in our conversation! Then, he responded by saying he agreed in principle; but he insisted that certain behaviors and beliefs would prohibit someone from going to heaven. To which I replied, that from a Buddhist perspective, we can experience heaven and hell within our daily lives, moving from one to another at any moment according to our interactions with our environment and with those around us. On this point, we politely agreed to disagree.

Finally arriving at my daughter's house, we hugged; he said I had given him some things to think about and I felt enriched by his sincerity and our conversation. So, that's what happened when a Jewish Buddhist and devout Christian met in a taxi!

Finding Old Ways to Communicate

I appreciate the ability to share vital information and coordinate organizational activities using email, texts and Facebook. But, as a result of some previous challenging interpersonal relationships, I have also learned that when it comes to the lively world of human emotions, blogger beware!

Daisaku Ikeda has said, "We live in the midst of a flood of soulless information. And the more we rely on one-way communication...the more I feel the need to stress the value of the sound of the human voice. The simple but precious interaction of voice and voice, person and person, the exchange of life with life."

There was a time in the 1990s, when no matter how hard I tried, I couldn't get along with one of my work colleagues, "Bob." Bob had a way of getting under everyone's skin -- especially through the tone of his emails. My responses, which seemed so innocent and compassionate at the time, only made him more antagonistic.

I chanted a lot about this relationship and received encouragement from my therapist at that time, Jeanne. She had me close my eyes and imagine that I was Daisaku Ikeda talking to my coworker. Instead of firing off a quick email response to yet another angry message that had landed in my inbox, I imagined Ikeda walking from my office down to Bob's and, using a very warm voice, asking him how he was doing. I realized then that this was the caring attitude I needed to manifest to help bring out Bob's enlightened nature. I felt motivated to chant to have this kind of compassion.

The very next day, Bob and I ended up waiting for a government official in a conference room. I asked him how his family was doing. He said his teenage daughter had been diagnosed with diabetes a year before and had been refusing to take her insulin treatments. This was causing his family a lot of stress. I mentioned to him that it was also a very difficult time for me because Most Beautiful One, my wife of many years, had recently been diagnosed with MS. With this heart-to-heart sharing, Bob and I went from a relationship built on distrust to one of mutual respect. I have never forgotten this experience and benefit.

According to researchers, seven percent of our communications is what we say, thirty-eight percent is the way we say it - rate, tone and inflection - and fifty-five percent is our body language before, during and after we say it. So, what we write to one another needs to be extremely concise to be correctly understood. E-mail, texts and social media posts are missing the crucial sounds of a human voice and the visual context clues that let us know what the sender is feeling and if the recipient is greatly upset, mildly peeved or encouraged.

It often takes person-to-person dialogue to understand someone else's true intention and to improve a negative situation. It is one of the ways I try to create harmony in my surroundings.

When I feel compelled to write an emotional e-mail or text, I send it to myself and reread it the next day before forwarding it to others. By taking time to reflect, I can ask myself why I don't just call the source of my frustration rather than slinging a one-sided written message. Such barbs are impossible to recall and can cause considerable damage. How can I know if the recipient really understood what I meant if I can't see or at least talk to that person?

It takes our collective wisdom to use the full spectrum of human communication channels to build healthy relationships, communities and organizations. So, the next time I have the urge to send some angry written words off into the World Wide Web, I will chant and make a phone call instead!

Be the Change

Many of the world's most revered spiritual leaders have embodied this sentiment. Mahatma Gandhi told his followers, "You must be the change you wish to see in the world." However, agreeing with this quotation is much easier than actualizing it. So, what does Buddhism teach us about this concept and how can we be the change we wish to see in the world?

The need to take personal responsibility for the future was a major message delivered by Nichiren to his disciples in 13th-century Japan. He spoke out fearlessly against the arrogant authorities yet was infinitely kind toward people of sincerity. The Soka Gakkai International (SGI), the largest lay organization of practitioners of Nichiren Buddhism with 12 million members in 192 countries and territories, is continuing this tradition.

Our external circumstances - the harshness of our environment - don't prohibit us from experiencing inner joy and being the change. Gandhi along with Martin Luther King, Nelson Mandela and the three presidents of the SGI proved that. The spiritual founders of most religions also excelled in spite of their situations. Millions upon millions of unheralded individuals affect this kind of change every day. But, as Nichiren told his disciples, "to accept is easy but to continue is difficult."

Another aspect of being the change is the importance of setting a course that benefits as many people as possible. Daisaku Ikeda has said, "To possess wisdom and compassion is the heart of our human revolution. If you have wisdom alone and lack compassion, it will be a cold perverse wisdom. If you have compassion alone and lack wisdom, you cannot give happiness to others. You are even likely to lead them in the wrong direction. You also won't be able to achieve your own happiness."

Several years ago, my Buddhist friend, Ronnie Smith, on his deathbed, encouraged me to be the change. Facing the imminent end of his life, this was the message or realization he most wanted to share. This is what gave his life meaning. And I continue to learn that my daily Buddhist practice along with positive action and compassion for others really does make a difference. It takes all three.

Rewriting My Story

In 2014, my chronic back pain made a surprise visit (note to self: be more careful lifting my granddaughter out of her car seat). Even though I knew that this was just another of life's many challenges, I started feeling sorry for myself. Eventually this spiraled into worrying about aging and all the violence in the world. Finally, I began to worry that I was worrying!

Daisaku Ikeda has said, "Even if you have problems, even if you have done things you regret, or have made mistakes, your whole future still lies ahead of you. If you can just keep moving forward, telling yourself I'll start from today. I'll start afresh from now, from this moment. Then a whole new world of possibilities will open up before you."

"Okay," I thought. "Time to get active."

I knew I had to tap my inner wisdom to find a way to gain a healthier perspective. First, I talked to a few Buddhist friends and also called my therapist, Jeanne. She helped my wife and me through some of our darkest times. She reminded me that I have a full range of emotions that change every moment. I don't need to overreact to what I'm feeling at any given time.

Of course, I don't like physical pain. No one does. Also, at some point, most people are afraid of getting older. So, I started to create a new story about myself called: Making the Best of What I've Got. For instance, I was able to get out of bed today with only minor pain - that's something to be grateful for. I'm also going to stop comparing what I can do today with what I could do in the past (I used to be able to do that...). In my new story, I enjoy the things I am able to do.

I began dealing with my feelings of vulnerability. What's going on in the world is very frightening. But I remembered that it's okay to feel sad. A Buddha (that's all of us!) experiences enlightenment in all ten worlds (hell, hunger, anger, learning, tranquility, rapture, learning, realization, bodhisattva and Buddhahood). For instance, Buddhism identifies the pain of parting from one's loved ones as one of life's inevitable sufferings. It is certainly true that we can't avoid this experience.

In a recent lecture, Ikeda said, "The most difficult aspect of the principle of the mutual possession of the Ten Worlds is being convinced that the world of Buddhahood is contained within the world of humanity -- namely, that is exists right here in our lives, in our ordinary bodies and hearts."

He also encourages us to "become a brilliant beacon, shining with joy and happiness and to live your life with confidence and courage. When you shine with a radiant light, there can be no darkness in your life." Clearly, the choice is mine.

I'm going to continue to try to make the world a better place. I'm also going to give myself time to rest and play with no judgment or comparison with others. The bottom line: I will try to pay more attention to the stories I tell myself and, when they're negative, re-cast them. Now there's something to write about!

Helping Students Worry Less

Last week I spoke to six local health classes (~200 high school students) about lessons I wish I had learned at their age. One of their biggest worries was knowing what they wanted to do for their career.

When I graduated high school, I was living in my car and, occasionally, a friend's living room. I had absolutely no idea what the next day was going to bring much less my future career. Then I ran away with my girlfriend and life became even more difficult to predict. Looking back almost 20,000 days later, I have lived a surprisingly rich, productive life filled with many obstacles and victories and, most important, no regret.

My brother, on the other hand, knew from a young age that he wanted to be a dentist. He pursued and achieved his goal. Now retired, he is providing free care to children all over the world. Both of us ended up with successful careers even though we followed completely different paths.

High school is a wonderful place to gather the knowledge and life skills necessary to succeed in college and/or the workplace. Uncertainty about your future signifies limitless opportunities. And your sincere efforts to do your best in the tasks before you will be the cause for future success. You may have peers who know what they want to do but there is absolutely no need for you to worry.

Anxiety happens when you think you have to figure everything out now. It is better to give yourself time to explore than to force yourself to make a decision. Both my daughters (a journalism professor and a litigation attorney) ended up in careers that are completely different from their interests in high school. So, take your time!

Of course, efforts I made to build financial security and take care of my health were important. However, I placed the most value on wisdom, inner resolve, self-respect & compassion for others. Without these, the physical and material results would lack meaning.

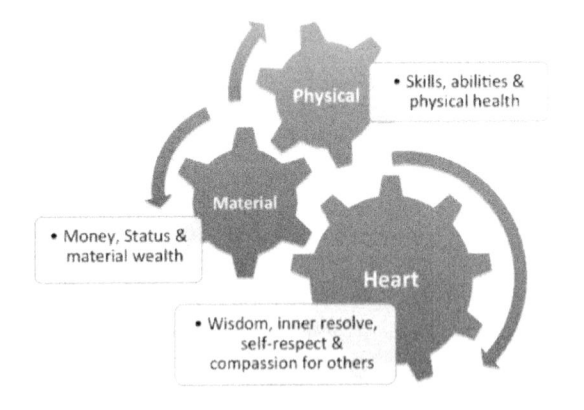

- **Physical**: Skills, abilities & physical health
- **Material**: Money, Status & material wealth
- **Heart**: Wisdom, inner resolve, self-respect & compassion for others

Psychologists are finding that people in their fifties and sixties whose primary focus in life has been the attainment of external material and physical goals, such as wealth, property, fame and status, tend to describe themselves as being less happy. In general, they experience higher levels of anxiety, suffer more from illness, and have less sense of fulfillment. So, it is important for you to seek out sources of inspiration and mentors while you are in high school. Take the time to strengthen your respect for yourself and others. These habits will pay huge dividends in terms of your future happiness.

Overcoming Ourselves to Help Others

I spoke to fifty high school leadership students about pressures facing them -- challenges like how to balance all their activities, how to avoid beating themselves up for making a mistake and how to improve the way they react to the events and people around them. As I left the school, I noticed many colorful chalked statements on the wide sidewalk like these:

> Don't give up
> You are loved
> We will miss you
> You are never alone
> Sending you & your family love

I was aware that a high school sophomore had taken her own life the evening before. Apparently, she had a history of depression. I recalled with the teacher that the girl might have attended one of the freshmen health classes last year where I shared my own experience with depression and despair. I spoke about getting help when you feel helpless and alone. This recollection caused the instructor and me to hug and cry. We agreed that the best we could do was to allow ourselves to grieve and then to refresh our determination to engage with each young person we meet in such a way that they would have a reason to go on living.

Daisaku Ikeda has said, "The experience of losing a loved one impels us toward a deeper understanding of life. Everyone fears and is saddened by death. That is natural. But by struggling to overcome the pain and sadness that accompanies death, we become sharply aware of the dignity and preciousness of life and develop the compassion to share the sufferings of others as our own."

A few months ago, while exploring some of my childhood demons and feelings of helplessness, I came across this reflection by Robert Harrap, the leader of our lay Buddhist organization in the U.K.: "When we are unsure of whether to behave in a particular way, perhaps there are some questions we can ask ourselves as we are considering what we should do, or how we should do it.... Am I acting with integrity and can I tell my family and friends about this behavior? Will this action create value? To what extent do I respect all the people who will be affected by my actions? Is the dignity of life at the heart of my action? What will be the consequences of this action?"

I heard at a recent study meeting that when asked what he felt his greatest accomplishment in life was, Daisaku Ikeda, soon to have his 90th birthday, replied, "I overcame myself."

As I continue to work on overcoming myself, when I'm emotionally struggling, I plan to:

- Chant to have courage, hope & purpose.
- Recognize the progress I have already made in my life.
- Focus on what I can do now to inspire others - not the entire state of the world.
- Study Buddhist & other inspirational writings.
- Play the harmonica, write, create art and enjoy nature.
- Be a loving, patient & supportive spouse, father and grandfather.
- Remember to breathe & exercise.
- Avoid magnifying physical pain.
- Remember that my earlier traumatic experiences took place in the past and only exist in the present if I let them.
- Always make time to speak to people who encourage me.

Creating Hope in Difficult Times

The deepest prayer of Shakyamuni, the original historical Buddha in ancient India, as well as Nichiren Daishonin, the Japanese founder of the Nichiren Buddhist practice in the 13th century, was to relieve human suffering. In other words, to give humans hope.

SGI members chant Nam-myoho-renge-kyo (pronounced repeatedly out loud as six syllables or beats: nahm-m'yoh-hoh-rehn-gay-k'yoh) and face their enlightened selves, which are mirrored in the scroll or mandala, called a Gohonzon, that we chant to in our own homes each day. The emphasis on audible chanting as opposed to silent meditation reflects a core aspect of this Buddhism. In addition to exploring our private inner life, our religion emphasizes the active practice of bringing forth our highest inner potential in relation to and for the benefit of our fellow humans and human society. Nichiren said, "The voice does the Buddha's work."

For Nichiren Buddhists, chanting every day is the engine that powers this active hope. It is how, in the words of Nichiren, "We become the master of our mind rather than let our mind master us."

This awareness or consciousness represents our true, eternal self. The revolutionary aspect of Nichiren

Buddhism is that it seeks to directly bring forth the energy of this consciousness -- the enlightened nature of a Buddha -- purifying the other, more superficial layers of our senses, our subconscious and our karma.

The word Nam roughly means to dedicate oneself. Myoho signifies the mystic or universal law. Renge symbolizes the Lotus Flower, which grows in a muddy swamp and becomes a beautiful flower. It also represents the simultaneity of cause and effect. Finally, kyo is sound -- a voiced teaching or sutra.

Nichiren Buddhism teaches that the self and all phenomena are one; all things are interrelated. In other words, all of us exist because of our relationship with other beings and phenomena, and nothing in either the human or the nonhuman world exists in isolation. It is for this reason that treating others with respect and dignity is so important.

Another fundamental premise of Nichiren Buddhism is that the condition of Buddhahood or enlightenment exists within each human being. This is why we don't focus on or worship an external statue of the historical Buddha, Shakyamuni. That wasn't his intention.

We all have the potential to be Buddhas, enlightened individuals who make a difference in the world regardless of our race, creed, sexual orientation or political persuasion. This is an ultimate source of hope for humanity.

Rather than exist in isolation by itself, this inner enlightenment manifests itself within our lives at the same time we are experiencing joy, anger, desire, tranquility, learning or the urge to help others. A man confined to a prison cell might find the inner strength and hope to take college courses and inspire his fellow inmates. On the other hand, a successful professional living in a beautiful mansion might be racked with emotional pain and anxiety.

This realization has had a tremendous impact on my attitude toward my life and the life of those around me. The act of polishing my Buddha nature every day has enabled me to overcome a painful childhood and build a happy marriage, a loving family, emotional health and a rewarding career.

Hope is akin to trust. If we could see it, there'd be no need for trust or hope. But hope is not avoiding what is going on in the world. Instead, fostering hope involves looking directly at our reality and making the decision to improve it.

The kind of hope I am referring to is not grounded in wishful thinking. In fact, powerful hope—what's been called 'active hope'—may not be possible without going through despair. It is during the darkest days that we need to persevere—trusting that hope is ahead.

When confronted by cruel reality, we need to create hope. We can do this by digging deeper within, searching for even a small glimmer of light, for the possibility of a way to begin to break through the impasse before us. And our capacity for hope can actually be expanded and strengthened by these difficult circumstances. Hope begins from this challenge, this effort to strive toward an ideal, however distant it may seem.

I believe that the ultimate tragedy in life is not physical death. Rather, it is the spiritual death of losing hope, giving up on our own possibilities for growth.

The problems that face our world are daunting in their depth and complexity. Sometimes it may be hard to see where or how to begin. But let's not be paralyzed by despair. Instead, let's each take action toward the goals we have set and in which we believe. Rather than passively accepting things as they are, we must embark on the challenge of creating a new reality. It is in that effort that true, undying hope is to be found.

Václav Havel, in his essay, "Orientation of the Heart," describes hope as "a state of mind, not a state of the world." Further, Havel says hope allows one to live with "dignity and meaning" in situations where both are in short supply, for example in his experience of Soviet suppression under seemingly impossible circumstances.

Recently, a friend reminded me that age is not an excuse for giving up. Allowing ourselves to grow passive and draw back is a sign of personal defeat. There may or may not be a retirement age at work, but there is no retirement age in life.

Fortunately, there is another Buddhist principle that regardless of the past, we can make a new pledge each day to learn from our mistakes and contribute to a more harmonious and peaceful society. So, every morning I try to renew my own determination and to remember as Gandhi said, "Good travels at a snail's pace."

Hope is a promise that the worst thing is not the last thing. This promise, that there is always a way out of the muddy swamp of daily life, can give us the power to proceed. And is what we mean when we talk about hope as a resource deep within us that has the power to transform ourselves and the world around us.

Through a persistent daily spiritual practice, we can manifest our enlightened nature. The choice is ours. And that is why we should never lose hope!

Dear Depressed

Dear Friend Who is Suffering from Depression,

I feel your pain. I spent most of my teens in the 1960s extremely depressed, took too many illegal substances, stole to buy them and was unable to function at school. I kept losing jobs, hung out with equally dysfunctional friends and almost ended my life. At 19 years old, I hit rock bottom and was desperate to change. Fortunately, my wife and then chanting entered my life.

Regardless of the labels society may give us, our challenge is to grab onto every positive support person and tool we can to survive and be able to feel joy and creativity in our lives. Some people have diabetes and need to take insulin. I need to take my medicine for my depression. Without these, I can't function in a way that enables me to experience happiness and help others. If I don't do the work, I can crash in a very scary way. My chanting has given me the fortune and wisdom to find the best professionals and the right treatment for me.

My Buddhist study and psychotherapy helped me to stop blaming my parents for their lack of parenting and to stop blaming myself for not being "whole" like all the other seemingly functional people around me. Like you, I've seen my fundamental darkness. But I also know that, like you, I have an enlightened self. I finally realized I needed to take steps to get healthy not just because my family wanted me to but because I wanted to. As a result, I have built a tremendously happy, productive life.

Please don't give up on yourself or those who love you. Our minds can be our biggest enemy. I don't believe 80% of what my mind tells me! There's a reason it is called a "mental" illness.

Trust your heart. Know you are an amazingly unique and creative human being who will find your way in the world. And you are strong enough to overcome your demons. So what if our childhoods weren't a Disney movie? So, what that it sucks that we can't take shortcuts...that we can't get stoned or drunk? Let's face it...we can't do these things any more than a diabetic can binge on sugar! By accepting the things we can't do, we can concentrate on all the important and wonderful things we can, including adding a spiritual practice to our daily lives.

I will never stop praying for your happiness. I will never stop believing in you. Don't waste any more time playing the blame game. It's just your mind playing tricks on you to distract you from getting better. Do what you need to do to become happy. I promise that like a lotus flower in a muddy swamp, your life will definitely blossom.

Overcoming My Fear

Multiple emotions co-exist in the place inside me I label "fear." There is the fear of loss, of discovering the truth about something, of never finding something or of being found out. I'm not sure if these fears already existed in my own mind or evolved as a reaction to the world around me. Maybe both.

Many times, while growing up, I found myself paralyzed -- afraid to take a chance, afraid to venture out into the unknown world. This emotional paralysis was based on the assumption that what I didn't know would surely harm me. So, I created a world for myself that was familiar and repeatable. I was afraid of other people, of being made fun of, of getting lost, of failing and of not being worthy of love. A lot of fear for such a small boy.

Sleep time was something I dreaded. During the day, I could keep the fear at bay by staying busy. But eventually I became too tired to play or read and had to go to bed. Out of necessity, I developed an anti-fear ritual. I checked under my bed for alien pods and all the upper corners of the room for deadly spiders. Then I rocked myself to sleep because it seemed to keep the monsters (both human and imaginary) from invading my bedroom and my thoughts. One particular nightmare of an electric alien from the movie Forbidden Planet was so powerful that it caused me to wake up sweating in the middle of the night. But I was too afraid to talk to anyone about it. Too afraid I would be laughed at. Fear often prolongs fear.

My childhood comfort zone was so small that sometimes I barely got enough oxygen to breathe. Even in my twenties, an overnight camping trip with my wife, Most Beautiful One (MBO), was a frightening experience -- for both of us. For me, because I knew I wouldn't be able to sleep at night and, for her, because she wanted so much to have a normal life with a functional husband.

I dealt with my fear of rejection by making light of everything. I reacted to the fear of failing by never quite extending myself. And I avoided "being uncovered as a fraud" by lacing my comments with self-deprecating humor. All in all, I became an expert at fear management. It wasn't until later that I developed the confidence and faith in myself to actually confront my fears.

Worrying about what might happen is very habit forming. I had spent my entire adolescence perfecting this ability. A useful protective device in my childhood, it was no longer necessary or productive. So, I decided to stop worrying about what "might happen," and concentrate on what "was happening." What a magical moment of Buddhist insight! I freed up an enviable amount of energy. Just imagine, I told myself, what I could do with all that time I spent worrying? After all, the terrible events I fretted about almost never happened. And when they did, I discovered I could overcome them -- becoming stronger and more fulfilled in the process.

Buddhism explains that my life and the environment are interrelated. The self or subjective world needs the insentient environment or objective world to exist. This suggests that my karma appears in both my subjective and objective realities. While two seemingly independent phenomena, they are fundamentally both part of my life.

When I first began to grasp this concept, it was tempting to merely blame myself for everything that was wrong with my circumstances, saying it was a reflection of my bad karma. But the liberating aspect of this concept is that since I shape my environment, I also have the power to change it for the better. It isn't intended to make me feel guilty for all that is wrong but to make me feel empowered to improve it. For the first time, I began to truly look inside myself for the solution to my problems.

When I look back at my life, I can see that every single meaningful experience was a direct result of some action I took. And these actions usually involved some degree of risk. Whether it was running away with MBO in 1969, moving from California to Virginia with our family in

1984 and then the two of us to an island in the Pacific Northwest in 2004, or starting my own consulting business in 1999, it seems that whenever I ventured out of my comfort zone, I began to "live better."

So, every single time I get up in the morning and chant, I take concrete steps to overcome the internal fears that used to paralyze me. I find tremendous hope in this.

Changing Mental & Karmic Constructs

A few years ago, I decided to concentrate on chanting to fundamentally change my relationship with physical and emotional pain. With the help of a wonderful therapist, I began to discover new insights into why the way I overreact is out of synch with my present reality.

Many of the mental constructs and habits I used to successfully survive my childhood stayed with me as an adult. For instance, I employed humor and self-deprecation in stressful work situations. Also, my tendency to rock back and forth, which was comforting as a child, made it difficult for grown up me to concentrate. It was as if my subconscious was still expending enormous energy reacting to past childhood events.

In many ways, my Buddhist practice has been a process of altering these subconscious habits and associated karma to reveal my true enlightened nature. By chanting through each relationship, health and work challenge over these many years, I have been able to slowly chip away at many of these unneeded defenses.

"Suffering only gets worse when we try to run from it rather than facing it." - Daisaku Ikeda

I'm now finally able to sit still without effort while chanting. This is also a tremendous benefit for my wife!

By letting go of these subconscious reactions, I'm more able to more easily elevate my life condition. And the result has been remarkable. I'm looking forward to transforming more past sufferings into joy.

Cells that Fire Together Wire Together

Neuroplasticity refers to the potential the brain has to reorganize itself by creating new neural pathways to adapt to changing needs. Or, according to my therapist, the more I practiced certain behaviors, the more my neural connections were changed and made to include all elements of the experience (sensory info, movement, cognitive patterns) -- both positive and negative. This is sometimes summarized with the axiom, cells that fire together wire together.

Please bear with me for one more sentence! Patterns of neurons that are used repeatedly to perform any function become connected in a way that makes the function easier to repeat and, conversely, harder to alter.

This concept helps explain why so many of my childhood behaviors such as rocking back and forth, feeling hopeless, and overreacting to pain stimuli have been so difficult to for me to change. It also sheds light on how my wife Most Beautiful One's (MBO) MS lesions on her spine disrupted her brain's ability to "wire together," resulting in her having to learn how to walk again.

Nichiren understood these challenges when he revealed the practice of chanting nam-myoho-renge-kyo. I know from fifty years of practice that this underlies and positively affects my senses, subconscious and karma. A very powerful unifying force indeed!

Applying my prayers along with constructive therapeutic treatments has resulted in more productive cells firing together in a way that has made new desired functions easier for me to repeat. Ergo...no more rocking when I chant, less worrying, and fewer dramatic reactions when old injuries flame up. And MBO's sincere practice and medical advances have resulted in eight years without any serious MS flare-ups.

Nichiren wrote, "Employ the strategy of the Lotus Sutra before any other." Our recent experiences have been wonderful examples of how our continued practice of Nichiren Buddhism has enabled us to find the right solutions for us and to get the most out of them.

A Great Path to Peace

In his 2016 (35th) Peace Proposal, Universal Respect for Human Dignity: The Great Path to Peace, Daisaku Ikeda states that all people have a right to live in happiness.

The United Nations has declared as its objective the building of a world free from the scourge of war, where human rights are respected, and discrimination and oppression eliminated. This vision is deeply compatible with our core values of peace, equality and compassion, that we, as Buddhists, uphold.

Too often our political discourse is infused with the mistaken belief that only certain groups of people have a right to happiness -- that their beliefs grant them special consideration at the expense of others. The problems that arise from this outlook can be overwhelming as can my own frustration with these negative attitudes.

Unfortunately, children often learn these behaviors from their adult caregivers. My parents were racially prejudiced as were their parents. And it embarrasses me that I once joined in teasing someone in junior high school about his speech impediment. On the other hand, I was treated badly for being the only Jewish student in one of the elementary schools I attended and, later in life,

Most Beautiful One and I were evicted from our rental home for having Buddhist discussion meetings. So, I have experienced both sides of these phenomena as an instigator and a recipient. Fortunately, I was able to embrace the practice of Nichiren Buddhism at the relatively young age of 19.

My Buddhist practice has taught me that all humans have the potential to be Buddhas, enlightened individuals who make a difference in the world regardless of race, creed, sexual orientation or political persuasion. This is an ultimate source of hope for humanity. Rather than exist in isolation by itself, this inner enlightenment manifests itself within our lives at the same time we are experiencing joy, anger, desire, tranquility, learning or the urge to help others.

Whenever I lost the belief that I could make a difference in the world I sought out encouragement from studying and having dialogues with fellow Buddhists and others whose opinions and worldview I respected. Then I chanted about what I learned and reignited my determination to put hope into practice.

In 2017, I gave a guest lecture on Creating Hope from a Buddhist Perspective (an essay in this book) at the West Seattle Unitarian Universalist church. It was a wonderful opportunity for the 150+ people there (including myself) to be reminded to self-reflect on their beliefs and behavior especially in light of the shootings that had occurred earlier that morning in Orlando, Florida. I continue to reawaken my own hope and respect for others on a daily basis with the belief that this is the only path that leads to lasting peace.

A Buddhist & Therapist Find Self-Love

I grew up in a neglectful lower middle-class Jewish American family where no one taught me I was lovable. This became crystal clear yet again in discussions with my new therapist, who I will call Kat (not Kathleen's real name). Yesterday, after chanting together for a few minutes (she's very open-minded), we launched into an exploration of self-love.

My parents, being somewhat self-absorbed and unaware, didn't really have a desire or know-how to parent children. What self-compassion pioneer researcher, Kristin Neff, describes as the human need for warmth, gentle touch and soft vocalization, was absent from my environment. As a result, I wasn't able to develop a sense of self-worth. At some level, I believed I was a sham and not good enough. I was able to feel empathy for others. But, with the exception of my wife and daughters, I had a difficult time fully accepting that I was worthy of love.

Many decades of practicing and studying Nichiren Buddhism helped me realize that I have a Buddha nature. By logical extension, I am deserving of respect and compassion -- especially from myself. To quote former SGI-USA general director Danny Nagashima, "When you sit in front of the Gohonzon (mandala) and chant, you have to have the most reverence for your life…your life deserves that kind of reverence."

While I knew this intellectually, there was a hidden, rooted in my childhood part of me that struggled to accept self-love. No matter how much success I experienced and obstacles I overcame, I still had difficulty embracing my most vulnerable and hurt self. In other words, loving myself flaws and all.

Kat explained how important self-love is to my mental and physical health since it is a powerful trigger for the release of oxytocin, the hormone that increases feelings of trust, calm, safety, generosity, and connectedness. So, I've been chanting to become a person who recognizes that I have an enlightened nature and am deserving of respect. She also shared how Kirstin Neff found that decreases in anxiety, shame, and guilt and increases in the willingness to express sadness, anger, and closeness were associated with higher levels of self-worth and a decrease in self-judgement.

In Judaism there is a ritual called Tashlikh where Jews cast off their sins into a flowing body of water. Instead of discarding sins, my daily ritual, based on the Buddhist concept of changing karma, is to chant to transform my negative childhood physical and emotional sensations into compassion and wisdom.

With a lot of help from therapists, fellow Buddhists, family and friends, I continue to find kinder ways to relate to myself. And, I believe I can finally say to that frightened adolescent me, with the utmost sincere intention…I forgive you…I will protect you…I love you.

When Teenage Angst is Not Just a Phase

Growing up in the 50s and 60s, the adults around me rarely discussed depression or mental illness. The few times I voiced a concern about my sadness to an adult, I was invariably told, "Oh, Michael, you just need to snap out of it," or some equally dismissive response. My parents, who were, in hindsight, extremely depressed alcoholics, refused to acknowledge my struggle as being anything other than childhood and later teenage angst.

I grew up too afraid and ashamed to talk about how hurt and hopeless I felt. Drugs became a self-destructive survival mechanism. It didn't help that I envisioned the mentally ill as being like characters in movies such as One Flew Over the Cuckoo's Nest. Who would want to join that club?

Starting at 19 years old, chanting became my go-to treatment for my emotional ailments. At some unconscious level, I knew I was depressed. So, Most Beautiful One (MBO) and I chanted our hearts out to prevent me from falling into an emotional abyss and to maintain a higher state of life. This worked for many years. I realize now it would have been even better if teenage or young adult me could have got professional therapy and medicine. But who knew?

In 1998, a few years after MBO became afflicted with multiple sclerosis (MS) and had begun to adapt, with a very positive attitude and daily Buddhist practice, to her new physical reality of increased fatigue and numbness, I could no longer control my emotions and was diagnosed by a psychiatrist as being clinically depressed. Even though this was painful to hear, I wasn't really surprised. I had always struggled with depression and anxiety as well as dangerous moments of total despair. I had a real fear of ending up in a mental institution although it was a relief to be told that I didn't have an imaginary illness I could just "snap out of."

So, I added psychotherapy and antidepressants to my regular chanting routine. 22 years later, I believe I have overcome the worst of my clinical depression. A lifetime of inner darkness has left the building!

It saddens me that so many young people I listen to or hear about are still reluctant to talk with their parents, teachers or friends about their serious inner turmoil. Making it difficult, is that these teenagers can appear to be relatively happy when around others. It was that way for me. I assumed the external role of being the "funny" one. In this way, both clinical and even situational depression can be quite insidious.

Almost all young people struggle with getting good grades, peer pressure, fear of making a mistake, and balancing school and extracurricular activities. Not having someone to talk to only exacerbates their stress. For some, this can manifest as serious depression and anxiety.

There are numerous other reasons why parents might miss or dismiss their child's emotional struggles. These include their teenager's resistance to talking with them; being too consumed with the drama and activities in their own lives to regularly communicate with their teen; embarrassed or unwilling to acknowledge having a teenager with emotional problems; uncomfortable with the terms depression and anxiety for what they see as just "typical teenage angst;" unwilling or unable to admit they might be contributing to the teenager's problems; or believing therapy and antidepressants are a "cop-out" and only for the very seriously disturbed.

Ironically, these same adults would never deny the existence of a young person's diabetes or suggest they not take insulin. They need to understand that the depression and anxiety that are plaguing their teenager are just as legitimate and treatable as other medical ailments.

It takes regular communication and compassionate intervention from parents, teachers and friends to prevent a teenager's angst from turning into violence against his or herself or others. Young people are precious. I'm going to continue to chant for the wisdom to self-reflect, stay aware and work with others who are struggling so we don't lose any more!

Moving Past Despair and Blame

These are truly difficult times. It is impossible to insulate myself from the divisive rhetoric and violent behavior occurring in every corner in the world. Believe me, I've tried! If I were to look down from the sky, I wouldn't be able to distinguish between the billions of humans living on the earth. Ethnicities, religions, lifestyles, and social status would just be meaningless labels. But, as has become so painfully obvious in the last few years, these labels actually have the power to really hurt people. Clearly these fear-based distinctions do not have the ability to create peace.

The Japanese word kosen-rufu is a Buddhist vision of social peace brought about by the widespread respect for the dignity of human life. The phrase first appeared in the 23rd chapter of the Lotus Sutra, the final teaching of the historical Buddha, Shakyamuni. He encouraged his followers to approach their Buddhist practice in a way that was actively engaged in the affairs of society as opposed to divorcing themselves from human desires and worldly affairs.

Over time, I've learned that my personal happiness is inextricably linked with the peace and happiness of my fellow humans. Enlightenment is not something to be only cultivated as a private, inner virtue. Neither is the goal of Nichiren Buddhism to garner reward in an afterlife. These two ideas are incompatible with the core Buddhist tenet that people are capable of realizing genuine happiness in this world as they are.

The life-state of Buddhahood is not a distant goal to be achieved after many lifetimes of suffering and practice. Rather, it is a condition of limitless vitality, wisdom and compassion -- one that is expressed and strengthened through committed action to contribute to the well-being and happiness of other people. All people have this Buddha nature. This means that every single individual is deserving of respect. To slander another is to demean and diminish my own life.

Kosen-rufu is about the struggle between the good and evil in our lives. For good to triumph, the evil must be brought into the light -- its true aspect revealed. I believe that has been happening all over the world and, hopefully, is a harbinger of an overdue positive global shift in how we humans treat each other.

Ikeda has said, "Kosen-rufu does not mean the end point or terminus of a flow, but it is the flow itself, the very pulse of living Buddhism within society." In other words, kosen-rufu does not indicate the end of the conflicts that drive history. Rather, it implies a world in which a deeply and widely held respect for human life will serve as the foundation for working out conflicts in a peaceful, creative manner.

I believe it is time to move on from despair and blame. There is just too much important work for us to do!

Feeling the Social Media Blues

"Goodness" can be defined as that which moves us in the direction of harmonious coexistence, empathy and solidarity with others. The nature of evil, on the other hand, is to divide people from people, humanity from the rest of nature. - Daisaku Ikeda

I enjoy social media. It allows me to stay connected to a lifetime of business and personal friends who might otherwise have fallen by the wayside. As someone who believes strongly that every life is interconnected, this is a real blessing.

Social media also provides a great avenue for me to exercise my funny bone as well as share my thoughts on life and the world. However, over the last few years, more people have turned to expressing their political and social views in strident and often overly aggressive ways. Besides being toxic to the people who write them, these words have had serious, negative consequences in our lives.

For a few years, I watched as many of my Facebook friends and people I follow on Twitter reacted to traumatic events in our nation and around the world. The unfortunate byproduct of this constant social media barrage was the regular re-traumatization of the original news events. So, I backed off of social media.

For three years, I worked with a therapist trained in EMDR therapy. She helped me process serious negative emotions and behaviors caused by my unresolved childhood trauma and recent disturbing world events that still want to push me in the wrong emotional direction. I am really pleased with the positive changes I have seen with this therapy.

This type of "processing" does not mean merely talking about it. It means setting up a re-learning state at the neural and cellular level that allows me to digest and, in a sense, change where I store experiences in my brain. The inappropriate emotions, beliefs, and body sensations are being discarded. And I am finding myself left with feelings, understanding, and perspectives that are leading to more healthy and useful behaviors and interactions. As John Milton, the English poet, famously wrote, "The mind is its own place, and in itself can make a Heav'n of Hell, a Hell of Heav'n."

I have also been recommitting myself to one of the basic tenets of my Buddhist practice -- that all people have the power to lead lives of great value and creativity. They can also positively influence their communities, society and the world.

"Nothing is easier than to denounce the evildoer; nothing is more difficult than to understand him." - Fyodor Dostoyevsky

Our lay Buddhist organization stresses that the greatest fulfillment in life is found in working for the happiness of others. I'm doing my best to use my writing and motivational speaking activities in local churches and schools to maintain and spread hope.

There is no such thing as an individual life or a world without challenges. Never has been, never will be. It is how we respond to these events that matters. And that's what matters to me!

Fifty Years But Who's Counting

Most Beautiful One (MBO): In June of 1969, at just 17 and 19 years old, Mike and I ran away from home. We were disillusioned with the "establishment" and I was forbidden by my parents to date him.

Mike: After months of hitching around California and living on a friend's porch, we began a daily practice of Nichiren Buddhism to polish our enlightened natures, overcoming numerous obstacles and consistently working to improve our relationship and contribute to world peace.

MBO: We were so fortunate to have embraced a spiritual practice at such a young age. Some of my many benefits include:

- Building a lifelong partnership with Mike against all odds – love triumphed!
- Having two wonderful daughters who cherish their childhoods and consider time spent with Mike and me to be their happy place.
- Completing college while our daughters were young to fulfill my dream and passion to teach.
- Challenging my MS from Day One and, as a result, developing appreciation for myself and others.

Mike: MBO went numb from the waist down in 1996. Not knowing if she'd ever walk again, I watched her deal with her diagnosis of MS with astonishing determination.

For my part, I discovered that when push came to shove, I was able to stand on my own and be strong for her. With the help of a compassionate therapist, I turned what could have been a devastating occurrence into the fuel to begin to make much needed changes in my own life.

Meanwhile, my love and admiration for Most Beautiful One continued to grow.

A few of the many life lessons we've learned are:

- Don't compare ourselves to others but rather express our own unique capabilities.
- See the enlightened nature inside our own lives and the lives of others.
- Nurture our relationships with dialogue - especially when we don't want to!
- No matter what obstacles we might face, never give up!

MBO: Over these many years, I have seen Mike really struggle with depression and anxiety. It has been so encouraging to watch him find the right medicine and therapists to help him heal from a terribly painful childhood. He has become much more centered and at peace with himself. It goes to show that we are never too old to change.

Mike: When we were first together, I played piano in a soul group in East LA. Now that I've retired from my consulting business, I've re-discovered my passion for music by singing and playing harmonica in a local blues band, Good Karma Blues.

MBO: I was able to overcome my mother's insistence that I wasn't her "artistic" daughter, by learning how to paint with watercolors and, more recently, to allow myself to experiment with abstract images.

We've also been enjoying time with our two grandkids and continue to host local Buddhist discussion meetings in our beautiful new home.

Mike: In 2003, we were asked to speak at our older daughter's friend's wedding ceremony at a stately old mansion in the western part of Virginia. It took us two weeks of reflection and dialogue to describe some of the lessons we've learned about marriage. Here's what we shared:

Communicate . . . set aside a regular time to talk,

But be flexible and willing to listen regardless of the time. Recognize and accommodate your different communication styles.

Don't go to bed angry, even if it means losing sleep to discussion.

Give your relationship constant attention.

Enjoy the good times.

Realize life's challenges will cause you to grow and deepen your bond.

Reach out to help others . . . it makes your own burdens seem lighter.

Love deeply and passionately.

Always keep your sense of humor.

Laugh together.

Celebrate each other's strengths.

Reflect on your own weaknesses.

Respect each other.

Act with compassion when your spouse is struggling.

Spend quality time together.

Yet give each other space to develop as individuals . . . it will make the time you spend together more fulfilling.

Remember that spiritual growth is a key component of a happy, life-long marriage . . . all the money, recognition and status in the world won't guarantee happiness.

Your marriage is truly a treasure.

And so are both of you!

MBO: We have spent many years working on improving our relationship. After we had our second daughter, someone pointed out to us that children learn much more about relationships from watching how their parents treat each other than from what parents tell them. I am thankful that both the girls have grown up expecting to be treated with respect and dignity.

Over fifty-one years of marriage, we've learned that in good and bad times it's most important to live with a Never-give-up-spirit. When we do this, "Winter never fails to turn into spring."

Being the Father I Never Had

"I feel that "treasures of the heart" are the greatest possible gift from parents to their children." - Daisaku Ikeda

I didn't realize as a child that my father was a broken man. Children rarely do. But sons and daughters are greatly impacted by the words, thoughts and deeds of their parents. His harmful actions (and my mother's inaction) affected our entire family. There were definitely too few treasures of the heart.

"The process of changing poison into medicine begins when we approach difficult experiences as an opportunity to reflect on ourselves and to strengthen and develop our courage and compassion. The more we are able to do this, the more we are able to grow in vitality and wisdom and realize a truly expansive state of life." - June 2002 SGI Quarterly.

We all make choices -- some more difficult than others. I have forgiven my parents for their unhealthy choices. Especially because thanks to them, I am here! The determination to be a better husband, father and now grandfather as well as a desire to be happy have fueled my spiritual journey since I was 19 years old.

A positive attitude wasn't something that came naturally to me. Fortunately, at its heart, Buddhism is an optimistic philosophy. So, every time my wife and I have faced a seemingly insurmountable obstacle, we've been able to rekindle our hope by remaining in the orbit of our Buddhist community.

There were times as a very young husband that I felt the undertow of my father's legacy. I had an almost visceral desire to run far away from my problems. But my awareness of the law of cause and effect served as a constant reminder that I was not broken; that buried under my childhood angst and confusion was an enlightened nature that could (and would) enable me to be a loving and committed partner.

Faced with the typical litany of challenges encountered by all parents -- childhood illnesses, temper tantrums, friend problems -- my wife and I repeatedly sat down to pray for the wisdom to make the best decisions for our daughters. I'm so grateful they believe they had a magical and nourishing childhood. And now my older daughter is doing the same with her children.

The younger me thought I didn't have what it takes to be happy. But now I know that through my Buddhist practice I can overcome any hardship and experience tremendous joy in my life. This confidence is my greatest benefit.

Can't ask for more than that!

Getting Comfortable with Discomfort

"Leave behind the passive dreaming of a rose-tinted future. The energy of happiness exists in living today with roots sunk firmly in reality's soil."
- Daisaku Ikeda

Dealing with discomfort has been one of my greatest challenges. As a struggling college freshman, I was living in the back of my Volkswagen Beetle when I met my wife. I fell desperately in love with her. It wasn't until we ran away together that I appreciated how committed she was to our happiness. And, while she was and continues to be a wonderful source of external support, the internal uncertainties in my own life and the world around me still practically paralyzed me with fear. Enter my Buddhist practice.

Nichiren wrote that Nam-myoho-renge-kyo is like the roar of a lion. During my most difficult times, I have been able to summon this power through chanting. It is as if my fundamental fear of discomfort is repeatedly replaced with hope, appreciation and a deeper understanding of my purpose in life. Because of this, I have been able to create a much happier life. However, it hasn't been easy.

"A passage in the Six Paramitas Sutra says to become the master of your mind rather than let your mind master you. Whatever trouble occurs, regard it as no more than a dream, and think only of the Lotus Sutra." - Nichiren, Letter to the Brothers

Having a fertile imagination is a double-edged sword -- the downside being the ability to scare myself with dream scenarios that are not deserving of any attention. These negative thoughts only add to my sense of discomfort and, if I'm not careful, can sabotage my happiness. My practice and several tools from my therapist have given me the wisdom to discriminate between make-believe and real problems. For instance, my mind will try to convince me that I'm depressed when I'm actually just tired. Discerning reality is often the difference between being mastered by my mind or mastering it.

Of course, there is a small part of me that still pines for a rose-tinted future. Holds onto the dream of an existence with no pain and no uncertainty. This misconception about human life can make it difficult to take the actions necessary to manifest my Buddha nature. And that is why Buddhism is an ongoing daily practice.

I'm a Buddha, You're a Buddha, Too

"Buddhism teaches that all people are inherently Buddhas. I believe that this Buddhist view of humanity embodies a fundamental principle for world peace. You are a Buddha and I am a Buddha. That's why we must not fight each other. That's why we must respect each other."
– Daisaku Ikeda

The universality of the Buddha life condition is perhaps the most important lesson of Buddhism. And yet it is also the most elusive. When I first encountered Nichiren Buddhism in 1969, I was a living testament to self-criticism, much of it directed inwardly as shame and outwardly as anger toward adults and the political establishment. My inability to believe in myself, while not surprising considering my childhood, was nevertheless emotionally crippling.

I found Ikeda's guidance, such as the one written above, to be consistently encouraging. It gave me hope and inspired me to begin what turned into a lifetime journey of self-improvement. Clearly, this was also the solution to the seemingly never-ending conflict that has existed forever between human beings.

I continue to try to avoid diminishing myself. After all, to belittle myself is to disparage the Buddha nature within my life. Whenever I placed someone else on a pedestal, as I was encouraged to do by so many organizations and the media, I inherently saw myself as being something less than that person. It's one of the aspects of our Buddhist community that I find refreshing; regardless of our ethnicity, sexual orientation and socio-economic status, we are all equal and deserving of respect.

There are many other aspects of this concept that we are all Buddhas. From an historical context, it is revolutionary. Just imagine if someday:

- People of every denomination spoke with mutual respect for each other's faith and differing religious beliefs.
- Political leaders from all parties and sides of an issue engaged in respectful dialogue, only responding after careful consideration of each other's point of view.
- Families celebrated or at least appreciated their differences and found common ground.
- Neighbors reacted to misunderstandings with compassion instead of animosity.

The list is endless. And reminds me that Buddhism is a teaching of the boundless potential within every human being. So, whenever I start to lose hope either in my ability to overcome my own problems or the world being able to learn to peacefully coexist, I return to this prime point. Because, otherwise, what's the point?

It's Never Too Late

Last night we had some new friends who were visiting the island over for dinner. I played harmonica with the husband, a wonderful guitar player. One of the songs he sang was a Steppenwolf tune, "It's Never Too Late." That got me thinking about some of the recent changes I have undergone.

Conventional logic would have me believe that at almost 70 years old, I can be comfortably set in my ways. But I've learned that from a Buddhism perspective, emotional laziness just isn't an option if I want to stay happy.

About three years ago, I read this guidance: "The fact is, when we support others, we ourselves are actually being supported; when we help others, we ourselves are actually being helped. This is the worldview of "dependent origination" taught in Buddhism."

The following day I flew to Rhode Island to be with my daughter and grandkids while my son-in-law was out of town. In the past, there was always a part of me that felt overly protective of my emotional space -- to make sure there was sufficient time for me to decompress. This caused my family to expend energy accommodating me.

So, I determined that 100% of this trip would be about helping my daughter.

My grandparents weren't present in my life. So, I have always tried to be a supportive, kind presence for my grandkids. Now it was time to take my determination to the next level. What a difference a subtle change in attitude and prayer can make!

For the entire trip, I was super patient Dad and Bubba (my grandpa nickname). And the most interesting aspect of this experience was that because I was so enmeshed in helping my daughter, she made sure I had some downtime. I also grew even closer to my grandkids. After the trip, she told my wife she wished I lived with them!

For some people, being able to concentrate on helping others comes easy. But because of my struggle with depression and anxiety, I have always had to make a concerted effort to move in this direction. For many years, I believed this would never change. Being able to now function in this way with much less effort is one of the greatest benefits of my Buddhist practice.

Enlightened Fatherhood

Note: This is an expanded version of a chapter in Romancing the Buddha.

Many years ago, when our daughters were teenagers, Ralph, a new father at work, asked me for advice about how to be a better father. I promised to get back to him by the next day.

My first priority was to find Most Beautiful One (MBO). Our many years parenting together had convinced me that if anyone could answer this question with alacrity, it would be her.

I located MBO at my younger daughter's soccer game. She was standing in the oppressive heat beneath a swarm of gnats the size of golf balls. Waving my arms furiously (these killer bugs hate soccer fathers), I asked her what single action I could take to be a better father.

"Simple," she replied as several screaming girls hurled themselves at our daughter on the soccer field. "Stop burping at the dinner table. It's a disgusting habit and it sets a bad example for the girls."

So, there you have it -- straight from an authority.

Somehow, while I had to admit she was right, I didn't think I had yet plumbed the depths of this issue.

Sympathizing with my obvious frustration, she referred me to something she had read by Daisaku Ikeda.

"All children are different, each possesses his or her wonderful unique quality. We must pour upon all children our great love and compassion so that each child can blossom, true to his or her unique quality."

That evening, as I drank a non-carbonated beverage at the dinner table, I asked my daughters the same question. Their numerous answers can be summarized as follows: "Mom always gets us things we need. Dad should buy us anything else we want." I wisely dropped the subject and hid my wallet.

Maybe, I thought, I should go to a more mature source of wisdom—my mother-in-law. If anyone would have an opinion about what a father's role should be, especially mine, she would.

Her response was actually very helpful. She said parents should expose their children to a variety of life experiences, because this gives them more choices and opens up their future possibilities. By a variety of life experiences, I suspect she wasn't including the fact that MBO and I ran away from home when we were just teenagers.

Having overdosed on family input, I decided it was time to get some Buddhist input. So, I called Carol, a member of our Buddhist community. She was involved in cooking eggs with her two small children. Our conversation was, of necessity, interrupted with shouts of warning, fear and panic punctuated with squeals of delight.

She said she thought a father, or in her case, her partner, Lynn, should feel the responsibility to protect her family. She also said she was recently encouraged to use her Buddhist practice to develop a calmer demeanor so she would rarely have to scold her children. When a parent scolds a child, it is very serious and should only be done when absolutely necessary and with utmost compassion.

While cleaning egg yolk from the floor, Carol added that she had learned that if her attitude and actions were correct and strong enough to make her partner happy, her entire family would be happy. She then quoted a song I have never heard on the radio, "When Mama Ain't Happy, Ain't Nobody Happy."

Later that afternoon, I played tennis with my friend, Bob. You can't top tennis in 90-percent Virginia humidity against a former college all-star for outdoor humiliation. In between beating me in straight sets, Bob said he thought the most difficult challenge for a father was allowing his children to be who they are as opposed to who he thought they should be. We agreed this was very difficult since we have such a strong personal stake in our children's futures.

I finished my two-hour imitation of wild gnat beating, and Bob helped me limp off the court. After a brief layover at his house for Band-Aids, I returned home to spend some precious time with my daughters. Later I read the following words in the Living Buddhism magazine: "What children expect of their father is neither the personification of profound knowledge nor someone with high social status, great fame, a prestigious job or top-flight education. They want a father with a good attitude toward life." That really made sense to me and, hopefully, Ralph, too!

In a letter to one of his disciples, Nichiren stated: "With regard to the debt owed to one's father and mother, the two fluids, red and white, of the father and mother come together to become your body. You dwell within your mother's womb for 270 days, a period of nine months during which your mother on thirty-seven occasions undergoes suffering that is close to death. And the pains she endures at the time of birth are almost too great to imagine, the panting breath, the sweaty steam rising from her forehead. For a period of three years you romp about the knees of your father and mother. So, when you come of age, you must first of all think of paying the debt you owe to your father and mother. Mount Sumeru is paltry in comparison to the towering debt you owe your father; the great ocean is shallow compared to the profoundness of the debt you owe your mother."

My own father pretty much broke every good parenting rule. It took a lot of years of chanting and therapy for me to replace my buried anger with forgiveness and appreciation. A difficult but critical attitude shift if I was to become truly happy.

In order for us to maintain and deepen our humanity, it is essential that parental partners work together in a spirit of reciprocity and mutual support. The relationship between them must be one of creative coexistence, based on the recognition that all things are interrelated. This is why treating others, especially our families, with respect, compassion and dignity is so important.

I've realized that every child wants a million dollars of effective parenting from their mother and father. Unfortunately, not too many parents have that much to give. Mine could barely manage a few thousand! MBO and I have always made it a priority to regularly communicate with each other about our children so that we are almost always on the same page. As a result, now into their forties, we have a wonderful and honest relationship with them.

I've also observed that when you stop complaining and when you stop making excuses, that's when you become an adult. This translates to fatherhood. A successful father never gives excuses or complains about his kids or their mother. Instead, he always takes equal responsibility for his children.

As a Nichiren Buddhist, I learned I didn't come from my father. I came through him. So, I got to choose the traits I wanted to emulate and those I knew I wanted to discard. This is all about taking responsibility for my own behavior. As soon as we stop blaming our own father and take responsibility for our lives and behavior, we can change. Children do much better when they have fathers who are committed to self-growth both emotionally and spiritually.

James Luther Adams was one of UU's most influential scholars and ministers. He believed faith is not fundamentally about one's beliefs but about one's commitments. Find out what someone values the most and you will have found the object of his or her faith whether she considers herself religious or not. Is it success? Is it the adrenaline rush of crisis? Is it comfort? Is it religion? Is it helping others?

Adams loved to say, "An unexamined faith is not worth having, for it can be true only by accident."

Authentic faith is an examined, self-critical faith. I believe this should be true regardless of our spiritual practice. Also, no matter what parental mistakes we may have made, Buddhism implores us not to be obsessed with our failings in the past. Rather it urges us to forge ahead with a from-this-moment-on spirit. In this way, we can make a fresh start every day.

When I turned fifty, my wonderful older daughter, a writing professor, wrote a fifty-word poem that I keep framed on my desk:

We scamper across mown grass.
Launched, the ball curves, dancing above our curls.
Night arrives: he shows us how stars form perfect patterns
And, more important, gently guides our palms,
His warm hand reaching toward the starry sky.
Back in the kitchen, pancakes fly – we laugh again.
Then, pouting, turn to homework and
learn to write, to present, to care, to achieve.
Lessons – easy, hard, observed, shown – and faith –
In practice, spirit, love and life – taught.
Adults now: we recall each squeeze, hug and talk.
Between us. Between them. They comfort.
Exposed to all conditions, we accept change.

He shares his sorrows and triumphs
Validating ours, freeing us to live.
At fifty, he represents everything we want to be,
Everything we hope to find.
He is home for us and for strangers.
The older we get, the more we need him.
Lucky us. He is our dad. Lucky Earth.

On Father's Day in 1999, I wrote a letter to myself that expresses the guidance and love I wish I had received from my father. (He had passed away a few years before.) The act of writing the letter was a very healing process.

Ikeda had this to say about raising children: "Some parents may wish to guarantee their children's happiness by giving them material wealth. Yet, no matter how wealthy they are, without good health and physical strength, children will not be able to lead truly happy lives. And above all, I believe that it is the "treasures of the heart"—inner qualities such as spiritual strength, character and humanity—that will ensure the true happiness of a child."

"If parents can raise their children in a way that discourages self-absorption and fosters open-mindedness, such openness of spirit will naturally develop into a warm-heartedness directed toward others, toward nature and toward the universe. And with such young people in it, I am confident that the world will become a better place."

I Was Never Happy Being Depressed

I carry on my shoulders the weight of generations of genetic suffering as well as my own childhood experiences. At times, the despair is overwhelming, and it is all I can do to just keep breathing. Fortunately, I embraced a spiritual practice at a young age. This has given me the energy and the hope necessary to continue to do my human revolution.

There are many theories as to whether mental illnesses such as clinical depression are inherited or a learned behavior. Most experts believe that our development is influenced by both nature and nurture. It is obvious from the actions of my parents and grandparents, that certain negative life tendencies were passed on to me epigenetically. As an adult, my choice became whether to play the blame game or take responsibility for the kind of person I wanted to be. As a Buddhist, the latter was the only viable alternative.

Still, during my most difficult times, it is a challenge to know what is real. The many joys in my life or the sadness? The confident me or the insecure me? The full me or the empty me? Perhaps each of these is equally true.

What I do know is that mental illness does not have to be a death sentence. Rather it can be the motivation for introspection and spiritual growth. In many ways, the blessings in my life are a direct result of this affliction. When I feel overwhelmed, I try to quiet my mind and remember that illness is an opportunity to attain a higher, nobler state of life.

My sadness has caused me to dig deep through therapy and Buddhist study to change as much of my negative karma into positive causes as is possible in this lifetime. In this way, I continue to chant and therapize for my own happiness as well as the happiness of my children, grandchildren and their future descendants. And to share my journey with as many people as possible in the hope that it might encourage someone else to never give up.

The Space Between Birth and Death

Lately, I've found myself thinking about the purpose of life. In particular, my life! As I approach 70 years old, I look in the rear-view mirror and see fifty years of marriage. I can see how my childhood depression and frustration led directly to Buddhism. And how the many times when hope seemed impossible, I was compelled to chant to raise my life condition. So, how do I want to spend the remainder of the space between my birth and death?

Buddhism identifies birth and death, along with aging and sickness, as universal or worldly sufferings. (Birth is a suffering because life gives rise to aging, sickness and death.) The Lotus Sutra, which Nichiren Buddhism holds as the core of the Mahayana movement, teaches that without the basic human impulses and the problems of life and death there can, in fact, be no enlightenment (explanation taken from the www.sgiglobal.org).

We've been studying the Opening of the Eyes letter that Nichiren wrote to one of his sincere disciples in the 1200s. What strikes me most is the importance of opening my eyes to the existence of my own internal Buddha nature. After all is said and done, it is only through this awareness that I can return to a place of hope and confidence in my ability to continue to change my circumstances. Something I have done repeatedly over the years.

In an essay on life and death, Daisaku Ikeda said, "Death does not discriminate; it strips of us everything. Fame, wealth and power are all useless in the unadorned reality of the final moments of life. When the time comes, we will have only ourselves to rely on. This is a solemn confrontation that we must face armed only with our raw humanity, the actual record of what we have done, how we have chosen to live our lives, asking, 'Have I lived true to myself? What have I contributed to the world? What are my satisfactions or regrets?'"

"To die well, one must have lived well. For those who have lived true to their convictions, who have worked to bring happiness to others, death can come as a comforting rest, like the well-earned sleep that follows a day of enjoyable exertion."

For the longest time, my biggest challenge has been sadness. Josei Toda once said, "Life doesn't always go smoothly. But everything has meaning. The greater the hardships, the greater the benefits. Firmly uphold the Mystic Law and strive your hardest, daring obstacles to stand in your way! Faith is the power to transform yourself and everything in your life."

Ikeda wrote, "I believe that in order to enjoy true happiness, we should live each moment as if it were our last. Today will never return. We may speak of the past or of the future, but the only reality we have is that of this present instant. And confronting the reality of death actually enables us to bring unlimited creativity, courage and joy into each instant of our lives."

Seven years ago, I spent several months learning how to play the harmonica. I was (and am) thrilled to have rediscovered the joy of playing music again. I am now equally convinced that I want to remain actively engaged through music and other creative endeavors to make a positive difference in the world around me as long as I can and in my own unique way. As Nichiren said in the letter entitled Happiness in this World, "Suffer what there is to suffer, enjoy what there is to enjoy. Regard both suffering and joy as facts of life and continue chanting Nam-myoho-renge-kyo, no matter what happens."

I think I can do that!

Discovering a Greater Purpose

When Most Beautiful One (MBO) was diagnosed with MS, it was a very scary time for our family. At the time, we didn't know if MBO would ever be able to walk again. But, just one year later in 1998, we did a six-mile walk to raise money for the National MS Society research and services. Everyone cried when MBO crossed the finish line. Eventually, to conserve her energy and manage her health issues, she transitioned from a full-time elementary school teacher to a half-time reading specialist.

Daisaku Ikeda said in a lecture that, "according to Nichiren Daishonin, there is the ultimate goal of life and various challenges along the way. The supreme and ultimate goal is the grand undertaking of kosen-rufu [world peace]. Once we are clear about our true purpose in life, we can create the best possible value from every challenge that appears along the way. When we are dedicated to realizing the great vow for kosen-rufu, we can transform everything without exception into a source for creating something positive. This is the true meaning of earthly desires are enlightenment and the sufferings of birth and death are nirvana."

This reminds me that kosen-rufu isn't only a long-term vision. It is also something I can actualize now in my immediate surroundings through chanting, determination and effort. That is the power of Nam myoho renge kyo.

In 2004, MBO and I moved from Virginia to Bainbridge Island, Washington, to live in a climate more suited to people with MS. That first year we met other people on the island with MS but most of them didn't know each other. Very few of our neighbors had any idea what MS was. The nearest annual MS walk was in Seattle, a 35-minute ferry ride followed by a 20-minute drive to the University of Washington football stadium.

After our first (and only) Seattle Walk MS, we determined to start an event on Bainbridge Island. We had to convince the local MS Society chapter that we could successfully organize a walk on the island. They were skeptical at first but decided to give us a chance. We weren't quite sure what to expect, but after a lot of work and community support, we held the first annual walk in 2007 with almost 250 walkers and collected $75,000. Ten years later, we had raised a total of $975,000 for MS research and services. After that year's tenth walk, we retired from our organizer role.

We joke (somewhat seriously) that our whole family has MS. Co-coordinating the walk was my way of expressing my support and love for my wife of over fifty years and to all the other families in our area who are struggling to make the best of a difficult situation. And while a tremendous challenge, MS has also been the impetus for my own human revolution.

The Pain is Mainly in My Brain

Like a gazillion other people, I went through several years of chronic lower back pain. Chronic meant my patient wife had to hear about it too often. It wasn't enough to keep me in bed, just enough to be a nagging distraction. And right when I thought it had finally disappeared, it would flare up again. Either from something like twisting the wrong way reaching for something on a top shelf or for no apparent reason at all.

My physical therapist, Mikki, made heroic efforts to help me understand that the pain I was experiencing was actually in my brain. In other words, my body was sending signals that my brain has chosen to interpret as pain even when there is no apparent threat. So it stands to reason that part of the solution to my chronic pain laid in making a fundamental change to the way my mind interpreted the data it received. While this explanation made intellectual sense to me, I still found myself picturing the pain as residing in my back.

Recent studies (L.A. Times, September 2013) have shown that there are clear differences that distinguish the brains of those with chronic pain from those without such pain. Chronic pain sufferers consistently show reduced volume in the brain's gray matter, the cortical structures key to perception, movement, memory and reasoning. Researchers have also shown that compared to healthy patients, the brains of chronic pain sufferers are wired differently in ways that suggest that physical sensations and emotional responses are bound more tightly together.

I have reduced gray matter! Who knew?

Well, actually Buddhism explains that the physical and spiritual aspects of our lives are completely inseparable and of equal importance. This is expressed in the Japanese expression "shikishin funi" meaning the oneness of body and mind.

In a 2003 article, Ikeda explained, "Our inner mental state also affects the physical functioning of our bodies. The most dramatic manifestations of this are laughter and tears, physical signs of our inner feelings. Mental or psychological stress has been linked to a range of illness from skin disorders, allergies, asthma and ulcers to cancer. Depression and hopelessness lower the body's resistance, making us vulnerable to a variety of afflictions. On the other hand, a positive determination to overcome illness can "inspire" our organs and even individual cells toward health."

I eventually realized that I had tremendous power in my mind to influence the effectiveness of medical treatments.

As Ikeda has said, "The key to battling illness lies in summoning a vigorous life-force and a positive fighting spirit. This brings out the full effectiveness of a curative treatment."

Are You Too Busy to Say No?

I once wrote an article about trying to focus my attention on helping others. I received many responses including a friend who emailed, "My problem is that I usually give so much of myself to other people that there is too little time left for me." This reminded me that for many people, saying no is a tremendous challenge.

Some people over-commit even when it jeopardizes their mental and physical health. In my younger days, when I tried to slow down, I would be overcome with dark feelings. So, I survived by saying "Yes" to everything and filling my schedule. Eventually, I ran out of gas!

Nichiren had this to say about the importance of uncovering the true aspect of our lives, a critical first step in developing the insight to make wise decisions: "A mind now clouded by the illusions of the innate darkness of life is like a tarnished mirror, but when polished, it is sure to become like a clear mirror, reflecting the essential nature of phenomena and the true aspect of reality. Arouse deep faith, and diligently polish your mirror day and night. How should you polish it? Only by chanting Nam-myoho-renge-kyo."

As a young manager at an aerospace company in the 1980s, my peers were working very long hours. Just for curiosity's sake, I asked different executives if there was anything in their career that they would have done differently if given the chance. Their answers gave me a lot to chant about.

Every single one told me that they wished they hadn't worked such long hours and that, in hindsight, they should have avoided bringing their work home. Because, as a result, they all ended up divorced and estranged from their adult children. I made a strong determination to make my relationship with my wife and daughters a priority.

With business travel and regular deadlines, maintaining a work-family balance was always on my mind. I once flew home to Virginia from Amsterdam just to catch one of my older daughter's ballet recitals and then took a plane back to London the next day to finish my trip. She never forgot that. I also made it a habit to leave the office on time unless I had critical work to get done as opposed to just staying late because others were.

As a leadership coach, I had many executives tell me that my biggest contribution was to help them learn to say "No." Basically, to understand work-life-health balance and the importance of setting their own and their organization's priorities.

There are many excellent articles on the Internet about how to say no. But the first step is to overcome the underlying fear and to grasp why it is important to sometimes take a pass. This one change revolutionized my life. And I suspect it will improve yours as well.

Stepping Through the Ten Worlds

Based on his reading of the Lotus Sutra, the sixth-century Chinese Buddhist T'ien-t'ai developed a system that classifies human experience into ten states or "worlds." This Ten Worlds teaching was adopted and

Bodhisattva, Realization, Learning, Rapture, Tranquility, Anger, Animality, Hunger, Hell, Buddhahood

elaborated on by Nichiren, who stressed the inner, subjective nature of these worlds, saying, "As to the question of where exactly Hell and the Buddha exist, one sutra reads that Hell exists underground and another sutra says that the Buddha is in the west. However, closer examination reveals that both exist in our five-foot body."

I am intimately familiar with Hell, the lowest of these ten conditions, having spent much of my youth there. It is characterized by misery, suffering, grief and destructive rage or depression. I'm grateful to have been able to chant to turn these experiences into life lessons that I can share with others.

Another lower life condition, hunger, is the experience of being dominated by one's desires or cravings, both physical and mental. I have found this to be a tough world to challenge. I have always craved a life free of physical and emotional pain. Of course, there is no way to be alive and never experience illness, fear or sadness. Now they have much less sway over my life than before.

Animality is an instinctive behavior lacking in reason. It can manifest as a fear of those who seem stronger and bullying of those who seem weaker. The more I chant and study, the less affected I am by other people's negative behavior. Practicing in the SGI has also helped me to learn how to have compassion for others who are different than me.

When my wife and I were first married in 1969, I had a fair amount of frustration and anger, the world of self-centeredness and ego. I once threw a chair into a wall and put my fist through the windshield of our car. Not my finest moments. But this frustration, mostly with myself, motivated me to keep practicing to the point where I rarely lose my temper (a great benefit for my wife).

Tranquility or humanity is characterized as constant inactivity, laziness, or passivity. I have too much energy to spend significant time in this condition. However, one of the results of my years of chanting has been an increased ability to enjoy the simple relaxing things in life without the need to always be busy.

Rapture, or Heaven, is a short-term gratification when one's desires have been achieved. I really enjoy my visits to this world of conspicuous benefits! Unfortunately, it is not lasting and can quickly revert to one of the lower conditions of life.

I love learning about our Buddhism and how it relates to other fields of knowledge, a higher condition characterized by a thirst to learn about life and oneself from others and from existing knowledge. I recently became aware that because I had chanted for many years, I subconsciously thought my opinions about Buddhism were more valid than someone newer to the practice. I'm so glad I have rediscovered the importance of humility and that everyone has something to teach me if I am just willing to listen.

Realization is the insight about life gained from our own observations and experiences. Fortunately, I now more quickly chant for wisdom and clarity than just relying on my intellect and emotions when I am faced with a challenge.

One of the major advantages of having a mentor like Daisaku Ikeda is to be reminded of the behavior and the benefit of being in the ninth world of Bodhisattva. I am so encouraged by the actions of the many people around me who continue to do everything in their power to help others even in a world filled with violence and distrust.

A Buddha is an ordinary person awakened to the true nature of life and who experiences absolute happiness and freedom within the realities of daily life. This brings us to a key aspect of Nichiren's understanding of the Ten Conditions or Worlds. The tenth world of Buddhahood exists as a potential within the lives of every human being. And each world contains within it the other nine. In other words, we all experience and live in the ten worlds.

Someone may reside in a hellish place, like prison, but experience the compassion of the world of Bodhisattva. When my wife first got MS in 1996 and was paralyzed from the waist down, we felt like our lives had been transformed into hell. However, with our Buddhist practice and the support of our fellow members, friends and family, we were able to also experience tremendous love, joy, compassion and, ultimately, many great victories including her being able to walk again.

The world we are currently experiencing doesn't have to define us. Because through chanting we can manifest our Buddha nature within that condition. The choice is ours!

Discovering My True Worth

"When I think back on all the crap I learned in high school it's a wonder I can think at all." - from the song Kodachrome by Paul Simon

Growing up, I was taught that my self-worth would be measured by my intellectual prowess, musical success and financial acumen. Unfortunately, as a young adult I believed I was sorely lacking in all three areas. I almost set a record for most times on academic probation at U.C.L.A., played piano in an unheard-of soul group, and lived in the back of my Volkswagen bug. Fortunately, Most Beautiful One (MBO) loved me for who I was inside. But I had a difficult time internalizing that concept.

My Buddhist studies explained in no uncertain terms that each human being, including me, was worthy of respect regardless of their accomplishments. Still, I wanted to prove to both our parents and myself that I was not a failure.

Of course, there isn't anything wrong with pursuing advancement at work or the respect of others. Where it gets tricky is when those human desires lack a deeper sense of purpose.

I spent my entire career in the aerospace and information technology field. As a practicing Buddhist, I tried my best to apply my inner wisdom and compassion to my work life. However, whenever I became too obsessed with being promoted, I would lose my focus and sense of appreciation for life.

In *Buddhism Day by Day*, Daisaku Ikeda writes, "It is important to remember that your worth as a person is not based on your profession. It is not based on wealth, fame or academic credentials. What counts is how hard you have striven in your chosen path, how much good you have accomplished, how earnestly you have devoted your energies to it. It is your spirit of devotion, your sincerity that determines your true worth."

Eventually, through chanting and much human revolution, I became an industry executive. I learned that life's challenges continued regardless of my position. Getting promoted was a nice treasure of the storehouse but not the source of lasting happiness or treasure of the heart. That had to come from within.

I came to realize that my real strength and passion was strategic planning and coaching others as opposed to chasing new business. So, in 1999 I took a leap of faith and started my own independent consulting company. I advised several hundred corporate and government managers until my retirement in 2016. It was a tremendously rewarding 17 years. Looking back, I'm so grateful for the encouragement I received from fellow Buddhists to chant and take action and to MBO for her continuous support (and amazing editing skills)!

Learning from My Mistakes

In 1976, I was the co-organizer of the SGI sponsored Bicentennial parade for the City of New York. We did a great job of delegating responsibilities, but I decided that only I was capable enough to lead the several cars carrying the VIPs including the governor to the review stand. Unfortunately, I hadn't taken the time to remind myself of the parade route, so I guided the waving VIPs past the review stand and almost all the way to Central Park!

After turning the cars around, I had to part several marching bands, drill teams and horseback riders to get the VIPs back to where they belonged. Truly a chaotic experience for all involved. However, I learned a valuable lesson about checking every detail of a plan and delegating responsibility as well as the negative impact of arrogance.

When I make a mistake, I feel a combination of emotions -- vulnerability, regret, dismay and guilt. These reactions are normal. I really don't like to disappoint people, especially my family and friends. The challenge is to find the benefit in my mistakes – like learning how to be more patient with others and myself.

Author Neil Gaiman has said, "I hope that in this year to come, you make mistakes. Because if you are making mistakes, then you are making new things, trying new things, learning, living, pushing yourself, changing yourself, changing your world. You're doing things you've never done before, and more importantly, you're doing something."

Now when I do something wrong, after spending a short period of remorse in my internal muddy swamp, I apologize. If necessary, I chant for wisdom, self-reflect and make a determination not to make the same mistake again. I then try to move on with my life. Allowing myself to dwell on the failure only lends it greater import. No one is perfect. And seeking perfection is a futile endeavor. Instead of bemoaning my failure, I set out to make brand new mistakes!

Relieving Suffering Isn't Optional

"The world remains beset by so much human suffering, poverty and deprivation. It is in your hands to make of our world a better one for all, especially the poor, vulnerable and marginalized." - Nelson Mandela

Relieving human suffering was perhaps the deepest prayer of Shakyamuni, the original historical Buddha in ancient India, as well as Nichiren Daishonin, the Japanese founder of our SGI Buddhist practice in the 13th century. One of the main reasons I was attracted to a Buddhist practice was to relieve my own considerable emotional suffering. Over time, I slowly came to realize the benefit of helping others -- that it was actually the most important way to polish my own Buddha nature.

So, when I speak about creating peace from a Buddhist perspective at different religious denominations, I can empathize with the many people I meet who express their frustration at the seeming lack of compassion on the part of people in positions of authority.

I think this situation is exacerbated by the extreme divides that currently exist between people of different faiths, political affiliations and sexual preferences. Buddhists believe that we all exist because of our relationship with other beings and phenomena, and nothing in either the human or the nonhuman world exists in isolation. It is because of this, that treating others with compassion and dignity is so important. After all -- we are all connected.

Too many leaders act solely for the benefit of the most wealthy and powerful at the expense of disenfranchised members of society or people who are not like them. They are acting out of ignorance of the fundamental premise that all people have the potential to be Buddhas, enlightened individuals who make a difference in the world. In other words, every living being is deserving of respect. Shouldn't this be the litmus test that every leader employs when making decisions?

I have to admit to struggling with this at times. I have to resist the urge to reduce people whose opinion I don't agree with to shallow labels instead of trying to understand their point of view. I am a work in progress!

Another universal truth is the strictness of the simultaneity of cause and effect. How would religious and political leaders behave if they understood that their very thoughts, actions and deeds will absolutely determine the quality of their own future inner lives? That there is no escape from this reality. This has revolutionized my own leadership perspective.

Ikeda stated in his multi-volume series, *The New Human Revolution*, "Let's remain convinced that each of our efforts to treat everyone we come into contact with understanding and compassion will make a profound difference in the world. It is exactly through making these efforts every day that we can reignite and maintain our inner confidence in the future."

When Good Enough is Good Enough

I remember when my brother, Markie (not Mark's real name), ran his first full marathon. He was so proud of himself for having crossed the finish line until our father expressed his disappointment that Markie hadn't come in first. This message that only the most perfect outcome is meaningful had a profound influence on both of us.

For my brother it meant, in spite of his many accomplishments, putting a lot of pressure on himself to do even better. On the other hand, I found myself reluctant to try new experiences in the fear that I would fail -- be less than perfect. Unfortunately, this meant missing out on opportunities for growth and enjoyment in my earlier years.

Nichiren Buddhism teaches that every human being is unique and worthy of respect. Eventually, I was able to overcome my earlier reluctance to leave my comfort zone and my tendency to compare myself with others. Instead, my measure of "good enough" became whether I tried my best given the circumstances. I replaced harsh inner judgement with appreciation and respect for myself.

Daisaku Ikeda has said, "We often hear people say they aren't capable. But this is a defeatist attitude. If you feel you aren't capable, then tap into the great reservoir of potential inside you.... If we chant to the Gohonzon [the scroll SGI Buddhists chant to], we can bring forth all the ability and strength we will ever need. "

At this point in my life, I spend most of my time writing, speaking about Buddhism and hope, and playing music in a local blues band. The reality that I can now engage in each of these endeavors with joy didn't happen overnight. It took many years of chanting and therapy to let go of the misconceptions that were preventing me from accepting myself as a "good enough" human being just the way I was as opposed to what others thought I should be.

Now, a combination of trying my best, chanting for my own success, and being satisfied with and learning from the result has become a great formula for my own growth and happiness. And that's good enough for me!

Each Child is Our Responsibility

All children are gems, full of precious potential. There is hope in every child since life itself is full of hope. Should the hopes of children be stifled or broken, that would be our responsibility as adults. - Daisaku Ikeda

As I speak to local high school students, it is obvious that their wishes and concerns are a microcosm of our greater society. For the most part, they want to build a comfortable, creative life for themselves and contribute to the happiness of others. They also struggle mightily with depression, fear and anxiety. As parents, grandparents and adults, I believe we have a moral responsibility -- an imperative -- to support each of these young people in any way possible.

Ikeda has also said, "When adults are ailing and their vision is clouded, children will suffer. Let us wipe the tears of sorrow from the face of each child. We must protect children and give them courage, strength and vitality. It is parents who nurture children, the hope of humanity. How noble parents are! What a great mission and responsibility they fulfill."

Most Beautiful One and I had a young man we have known for several years over for dinner. He expressed many of his concerns and we shared some of the valuable lessons we have learned over the years. We've decided to make this type of activity a regular part of our life. After all, when it comes to the children of the world, we are all parents.

I hope we can each look for ways to be an emotional safety net for these wonderful future leaders of the world. Let's give them hope. Let's let them know that someone cares about them. Let's not let even a single young person fall by the wayside. For us adults, they are the gift that keeps on giving.

Tricking Your Mind, Not Your Karma

From the very beginning of our Buddhist practice, Most Beautiful One (MBO) and I were encouraged to chant a lot every day. We were assured that this would help us change our karma, accumulate fortune and realize our dreams. Since Nam-myoho-renge-kyo is the ninth consciousness, by chanting we can illuminate and change our karma (the eighth consciousness) and our subconscious (the seventh).

We took this advice to heart and, from the very beginning, chanted almost every day. This enabled us to challenge major obstacles like my depression and MBO's MS. Over the years, our chanting, like a savings account, has enabled us to more quickly overcome problems in the same way that it is much easier to accelerate a train that is already moving than a train that has fully stopped.

One of the aspects of practicing in the SGI that I like is that no one tells us how much or how often to chant. Instead we are solely responsible for the quality and quantity of our own daily practice. Likewise, we don't have a concept of guilt. Instead, we can learn from both our successes and mistakes and then make new determinations. But this doesn't mean we will get the effects we desire without making the necessary causes. Oh, if that were only the case!

If chanting every day is the engine, then faith and study have been the fuel for our continued growth and development. However, without chanting, faith and study would have been merely mental constructs. It is through sincere chanting that we have continued to change our negative karma to achieve positive results.

As a child and teenager, I took jazz piano lessons and played in a soul group in Los Angeles. I dreamed of being a rock musician and writer. Then MBO and I left home and were introduced to this practice. At just 19 and 18, getting jobs and an education, introducing others to the practice, and learning how to communicate with each other were our most important objectives. So, I put music and writing aside with little expectation that either would enter my life again.

Twenty years later, I began writing articles for the World Tribune newspaper, published several books, and was hired to pen a regular business column. Flash forward 30 more years, and after a successful consulting and writing career, I'm now playing harmonica and singing in a blues band, Good Karma Blues! While I was focused elsewhere, my daily chanting made room for all my dreams to come true.

There are hundreds of reasons not to chant each morning. In some instances, this makes sense. But, over the long haul, being an SGI member without having a consistent daily practice is like being a member of a gym without regularly exercising and then being disappointed with the results. Just another example of how we can trick our mind, but not our karma.

When Past, Present & Future Collide

"Present effects are due to karmic causes from the past. However, future effects arise from the causes we make in the present. It is always the present that counts." - Daisaku Ikeda

For most of my adult life, I've sought external validation. Most likely to compensate for the deep seated "you're not good enough" effects of my dysfunctional childhood. Yet, I am very aware that Buddhism encourages its followers to believe in their Buddha or enlightened nature – 'to concern oneself with the present and the future,' as opposed to living in the past. Clearly a meaningful goal. But those stubborn early negative experiences can easily hinder my ability to have compassion for myself and to be in the moment.

Especially for the last several years, I've been exploring what my life what would be like if the validation of my worth as a human being came from within. In other words, how would I feel if I were to truly embrace and integrate those early experiences and associated emotions that are no longer my current reality. In this way, I am witnessing how the past, present and future can collide. It's what I choose to do with this collision that will determine the outcome. After all, finding inner peace and happiness is exactly why I started this spiritual journey so many years ago.

This isn't a painless journey! As I have given permission for these buried feelings to see the light of day, I have experienced a corresponding fear and sadness. But I am also noticing an inner satisfaction with myself that doesn't depend on the opinion of others.

I am confident that as long as I continue to practice Buddhism, I will do my human revolution and learn how to only suffer what is necessary to suffer in this present moment which, I'm finding, leaves ample room for happiness. It is this struggle that allows me to find meaning in the crazy world in which we live.

I Won't Be Afraid

"Bravely overcoming one small fear gives you the courage to take on the next. It takes courage to become happy - courage to remain true to one's convictions, courage not to be defeated by one's weaknesses and negativity, courage to take swift action to help those who are suffering." - Daisaku Ikeda

I have had a fear of travel since I was a child. My bedroom was safe. Anywhere else was scary. When I was 12 years old, my parents convinced me to attend a sleepover camp. I couldn't enjoy the daytime activities because I was so anxious about having to sleep in a strange bed surrounded by other kids. Sure enough, I lay there all night without sleeping. I had my older sister pick me up the next morning.

This anxiety (and depression) carried through to the early years of my marriage. I am still filled with wonder that Most Beautiful One (MBO) stayed with me as I struggled with being able to take family vacations. Fortunately, I slowly began to challenge my reluctance to expand my horizons.

According to Psychology Today, "Fear is a vital response to physical and emotional danger - if we didn't feel it, we couldn't protect ourselves from legitimate threats. But often we fear situations that are far from life-or-death, and thus hang back for no good reason. Bad experiences can trigger a fear response within us that is hard to quell. Yet exposing ourselves to our personal demons is the best way to move past them."

My SGI youth activities were a perfect proving ground for overcoming my childhood fears. I could test my ability to function in new environments without worrying about being judged by others. I spent my twenties marching in the Brass Band, watching over our Buddhist Centers and traveling to different cities as a young men's leader. My daily chanting helped me begin to overcome the internal demons that had prevented me from enjoying new experiences.

Our three-week trip to Spain two years ago was another conspicuous benefit of doing this human revolution. I truly had a wonderful experience. I looked forward to each day without trepidation. I wasn't even afraid when I drove on narrow winding roads to get to a picturesque village on the Mediterranean Sea.

Another aspect of our life that has impacted our ability to travel is the fatigue MBO experiences from her MS. For instance, she needs to rest for a few weeks after we visit our grandchildren on the East Coast. On a trip to Italy with our daughters over twenty years ago, MBO didn't yet know how to accommodate her MS and ended up collapsing in the street while experiencing anxiety and extreme fatigue.

So, we determined not to let her MS or my fear prevent us from taking our "bucket list" trip to Spain. This time I respected her boundaries by not being overly protective and she used self-awareness in choosing our excursions. We created the perfect vacation experience for ourselves, thoroughly enjoying the amazing Spanish museums, food and people.

I would like to encourage anyone who is struggling with fear to persevere. I have found these words of Nichiren to always be true: "Though one might point at the earth and miss it, though one might bind up the sky, though the tides might cease to ebb and flow and the sun rises in the west, it could never come about that the prayers of the practitioner of the Lotus Sutra would go unanswered."

Rub-a-dub-dub, Too Much in My Tub!

Like most people, when life becomes too uncomfortable, I can feel hopeless. Australian pain expert David Butler likes to use the analogy of a bathtub when describing the various "monsters" (negative and positive stressors) in our lives. These pressures can include physical and emotional pain, relationship issues and world events. When there are too many challenges to fit in the tub, our pain can become overwhelming.

Butler has shared that: We will experience pain when our credible evidence of danger related to our body is greater than our credible evidence of safety related to our body. Equally we won't have pain when our credible evidence of safety is greater than our credible evidence of danger (Moseley and Butler 2015, p. 14).

Fortunately, my Buddhist perspective has continued to enable me to bring forth the wisdom, courage and compassion necessary to transform feelings of danger into evidence of safety. A key realization is that I have the internal ability to modulate the degree of emotional or physical pain I experience at any given moment and turn poison into medicine. In this way, Buddhism and the science of pain have clearly intersected.

This awareness didn't come easy. There were times when the accumulated effects of my emotional and physical injuries and current events overwhelmed my system. And I learned that even positive activities that required my attention also added to the water level in my tub.

The first step was to chant and study Buddhist principles to understand that, as Daisaku Ikeda has said, "Ultimately, it is not difficult circumstances that defeat one, but one's own weakness." Also, to realize that I have a Buddha nature and the power to change my negative circumstances.

Next was to take constructive steps to improve my attitude and perspective about my situation. This usually started with discussions with Most Beautiful One, fellow Buddhists, a trusted physical therapist, and a psychotherapist.

I started learning how to more quickly seek out "evidence of safety" related to my mind and body. For instance, remembering that my depression never lasted and that physical injuries healed over time. It helps to understand that there will always be monsters in my tub. That's just part of being alive. So, now I go out of my way to avoid putting myself in situations that I know from experience can cause my tub to overflow.

So, rub-a-dub-dub, I hope you don't have too much in your tub!

What is True Happiness?

Note: I thought I would end with this lecture that I've given at numerous churches of different denominations over the last five years.

When we became Buddhists, my wife and I were teenage hippies. On the day of her high school graduation, we took a huge risk and ran away from home seeking love, peace, happiness and, in my case, freedom from responsibility. After months of eating brown rice and lentils and living on a friend's porch, we realized that we couldn't just survive on our ideals. Buddhism seemed like the perfect solution. We were told that if we chanted, we could become happy and all our dreams would come true.

I rarely thought to ask what true happiness was. I figured anything would be better than the severe depression and anguish I had suffered as a child and teenager. Because of my intense desire to avoid depression, I developed an underlying belief that the true objective of my Buddhist practice was to be happy all the time. That the enlightenment Nichiren spoke about was somehow wrapped up in an unshakable condition of happiness, a total absence of pain. "Look at me," I would be able to proclaim. "Nothing can upset my positive, upbeat attitude."

I was so frightened whenever I started to feel blue that I would do anything to get my smile back. My unhappiness, like a strong ocean undertow, was a constant impetus to chant more to strengthen my life. And, over time, I could make and carry out strong determinations, have a warm loving family, and build a successful business career. But, on a different level, I still needed to deal with the reality of my sadness. Soon, two traumatic occurrences pushed me right over the edge.

The first was the suicide of my good friend, Gordon, in the mid-nineties. He had been my business mentor and had recently retired. His family and friends thought they knew him well. A successful businessman, he was always cheerful and full of great advice. It frightened me that he could be harboring such overwhelming anguish that he saw no way to continue living. Obviously, he hadn't dealt with some significant issues in his life. Considering my own difficult past, I began to wonder if I was in danger of making the same mistake.

The second event was my wife being diagnosed in 1996 with MS. This was a challenging time that tested and then reinforced our commitment to each other and our continued spiritual practice. Eventually, Most Beautiful One (MBO) learned to walk again and some of the pressure we had been under was relieved. We had each gone through tremendous personal growth because of this experience. However, about a year later, MBO discovered me lying in the bathtub, unable to move. I had fallen into an extremely depressed state, the kind of loneliness and helplessness I had experienced as a child and teenager.

It was at this point in my life that I began to understand the kind of grief that must have driven Gordon to end his life. It woke me up to the need to get help. How sad and ironic that Gordon's most significant gift to me ended up being his death. His suicide, like a persistent flashing red reminder, compelled me to find the courage to "do the work."

Buddhism teaches that we should not shrink from the fact of death but squarely confront it. Our contemporary culture has been described as one that seeks to avoid and deny the fundamental question of our mortality. It is the awareness of death, however, that compels us to examine our lives and to seek to live meaningfully. Death enables us to treasure life; it awakens us to the preciousness of each shared moment. In the struggle to navigate the sorrow of death, we can forge a radiant treasure of fortitude in the depths of our being. Through that struggle, we become more aware of the dignity of life and more readily able to empathize with the suffering of others.

With my chanting as a spiritual foundation and a terrific therapist, I was finally able to begin the painful but rewarding process of healing myself from the effects of my difficult childhood, so that I could truly devote myself to living in the present. In the same way (MBO) took medicine and went to a neurologist for her illness, I took medicine and went to a psychotherapist for mine.

This wasn't and still isn't an easy process. I've had to push myself through many tears and painful memories. I discovered that the messages I assimilated as a child from an angry, deviant father and a disengaged mother greatly influenced my opinion of myself. As an adult, many of the behaviors that had protected me in my early years were no longer necessary or desirable. Nor were they contributing to my true happiness.

As part of learning how to deal with PTSD, I have also been learning to allow myself to feel joy without fear or guilt and to experience pain without panic. The essence of this is being able to live in the moment -- something we are taught as Buddhists but that can be very difficult to achieve.

The ever-present heaviness that plagued me for so many years has significantly diminished. There is no way to describe how wonderful this makes me feel. It is proof that it is never too late to change our lives. And, that many of life's treasured gifts are buried in the most painful and risky places.

I am so grateful that I could turn Gordon's death into such a meaningful gift. I'm reminded of one of my favorite quotes by Buddhist scholar, Daisaku Ikeda:

"Happiness is being able to experience profound joy that comes from never being defeated by any problems in life. In fact, these challenges are a catalyst to deepen and expand our inner lives. Despite a culture of instant gratification that influences so much of modern living, happiness is not a quick fix attained overnight. Rather, it results from our daily efforts to manifest life's highest potentials—wisdom, compassion, courage and vitality."

While pursuing happiness, I also used to spend considerable energy trying to reach an elusive "there," "there" meaning everything "good" -- a better job, a more pleasant boss or just a little more money. It was almost impossible to enjoy life as it was, when I was so busy wishing I were somewhere else. This also is not true happiness!

The belief that our happiness depends on some event or situation happening in the future sets us up for unhappiness. Especially when we consider that we are all bound by the cycle of birth, sickness, old age and death. If we wait for a trouble-free life, our happiness will continue to elude us. Rather, the question is how do we respond when confronted with the problems we will inevitably face? Eventually I came to realize that true happiness is when I strive to do my human revolution – those efforts I make to overcome myself and to help others.

While financial and material wealth is desirable, it is the nature of our attachment to it that can become problematic. In other words, does our attachment create value in our lives – does it contribute to our own and others' absolute happiness or is it just a lesser relative happiness? Through my many years of Buddhist practice, I've come to realize it is spiritual wealth, the inner treasures of the heart, that really guide us to true happiness.

Ikeda also said, "The gratification of desires is not happiness. Genuine happiness can only be achieved when we transform our way of life from the unthinking pursuit of pleasure to one committed to enriching our inner lives, when we focus on "being more rather than simply having more."

In the sixth century, a Buddhist scholar in China, T'ien-t'ai, identified ten worlds -- ten states or conditions of life that we experience within our lives, moving from one to another at any moment according to our interactions with our environment and those around us. These conditions are hell, hunger, animality, anger, tranquility, rapture, learning, realization, Bodhisattva and Buddhahood. Each of us possesses the potential to experience all ten, from the prison-like despair and self-hatred of Hell to the expansive joy and wisdom of Buddhahood. We each usually have one of these states that we revert to when faced with a stressful situation.

Any happiness or satisfaction to be gained in the lower six states depends totally on unique external circumstances and is therefore transient and subject to change. And, if we're not careful, risks taken while in these conditions of life will not have a positive effect. This is not true happiness.

The seventh and eighth states, Learning and Realization, come about when we recognize that everything experienced in the six paths is impermanent, and we begin to seek some lasting truth. Seeking the truth implies going out of our comfort zone to experience personal growth. However, since these states are self-focused, there is a great potential for egotism.

The ninth state of Bodhisattva indicates those who aspire to achieve enlightenment and at the same time are equally determined to enable all other beings to do the same. Those in this state find their greatest satisfaction in altruistic behavior. The risk we take to help others results in the deepest personal happiness.

The state of Buddhahood represents an ordinary person awakened to the true nature of life – one who experiences absolute happiness and freedom, not separate from but within the realities of daily existence – in other words within the other nine conditions of life. It is characterized by wisdom, compassion, creativity and life force. So, the objective is to bring out the enlightened, positive aspects of whatever circumstances we find ourselves in. This is, from a Buddhist perspective, true happiness.

In other words, the condition of Buddhahood does not exist separate from our daily life. We can experience joy in a hellish prison or transform our anger to engage in a risky but crucial fight against injustice. We don't need to be a victim of our circumstances.

The revolutionary aspect of Nichiren Buddhism is that it seeks to directly bring forth the energy of the enlightened nature of a Buddha to purify the other, more superficial layers of our five senses, our subconscious and our karma. It is how, in the words of Nichiren, "We become the master of our mind rather than letting our mind master us."

Chanting is the engine that enables us to reveal our Buddha nature. Chanting some strange words may be outside many people's comfort zone. However, the positive reward far outweighs the risk of giving it a try.

Consistent with our Buddhist concept of relative and absolute happiness, psychological research has also found that people in their later years whose primary focus in life has been the attainment of external goals such a wealth, property, fame and status - tend to be less happy. In general, they are said to experience higher levels of anxiety, suffer more from illness, and have less of a sense of fulfillment. On the other hand, people who have paid attention to treasures of the heart – their spiritual well-being – report being much more satisfied with their lives.

In the Progress Paradox, Gregg Easterbrook draws upon three decades of wide-ranging research to make the assertion that while almost all material and physical aspects of Western life have vastly improved in the past century, most people feel less happy than in previous generations. So, while pursuing physical and material fulfillment, what is most important is to develop the ability to make wise decisions, the courage to never give up, respect for oneself and compassion for others. These are the attributes that give real meaning to our external endeavors and accomplishments.

In a fascinating paper in the 2017 International Journal of Wellbeing, psychologist Ashley Buchanan proposes bringing together two areas of research – a "being well" perspective from positive psychology and a socially and ecologically orientated "doing good" perspective.

He gives the example of benefit mindset as everyday leaders who seek to "be well" and "do good." Wouldn't that be refreshing? It is interesting to note that this is in complete accord with the teachings of Nichiren which emphasize the need to practice every day for the happiness of oneself and others.

In the July 2, 2013 Psychology Today, well-being researchers Robert Biswas-Diener and Todd Kashdan stated, "While we don't deny the importance of happiness—we've also concluded that a well-lived life is more than just one in which you feel "up." The good life is best construed as a matrix that includes happiness, occasional sadness, a sense of purpose, playfulness, and psychological flexibility, as well autonomy, mastery, and belonging."

Personally, I believe true happiness is something close to the joy or sense of fulfillment and confidence that arises from our sense of mission to make the world a better place and from the ability to enjoy our life. Being happy is a sense of connectedness with everything around us. And, as Ikeda has said, "Happiness is not found in a tranquil life free of storms and tempests. Real happiness is found in the struggles we undergo to realize our goals, in our efforts to move forward."

Now I realize we don't really believe that if people chant or meditate or pray, they will always be smiling and cheerful. Rather, they will be more fulfilled and happier with their lives. Lasting happiness comes from within and is a condition we can experience even when or because we're facing difficulties. To quote Ralph Waldo Emerson, "Don't be too timid and squeamish about your actions. All life is an experiment. The more experiments you make the better."

Even amidst the most trying times, happiness is not out of reach. By accepting small risks, we can move in the direction of our dreams and face our problems wisely and courageously. We can come to savor the greatest of all joys: the ability to live life with a deeper and stronger sense of confidence, appreciation and hope. We have the power to take charge of our own destiny and become a source of positive change in our family, local community and the entire world.

In today's challenging times, it helps me to remember that happiness, like hope, is truly the state of my mind, not the state of the world. This truth gives me confidence that each of us can build a happy life and make a positive difference in the world.

For Further Information

- Books at MiddlewayPress.org
- Over 100 books written or co-authored by Daisaku Ikeda
- SokaGlobal.org (Soka Gakkai International – in 192 countries and territories)
- SGI-USA.org (with over 3,500 local discussion meetings in American members' homes and ~100 Buddhist Centers)
- *Romancing the Buddha* (3rd edition - available on Amazon.com)

Glossary of Buddhist Terms

Buddhism and Buddha—Buddhism is the name given to the teachings of the first historical Buddha (see Shakyamuni). In other words, Buddhism refers to all the sutras that Shakyamuni Buddha expounded in what is today called India in approximately 500 BCE. Nichiren's teachings (thirteenth century Japan) are referred to as the Buddhism of sowing, in contrast with the earlier teachings of Shakyamuni, which are called the Buddhism of the harvest. The Buddhism of the harvest is that which can lead to enlightenment only for those who received the seeds of Buddhahood by practicing the Buddha's teachings in previous lifetimes. In contrast, the Buddhism of sowing implants the seeds of Buddhahood, or Nam-myoho-renge-kyo, in the lives of those who had no connection with the Buddha in their past existences.

The Buddha can in no way be defined as a transcendental or supreme being. "Buddha" means the Enlightened One; Buddha is a person who perceives within his own life the essence or reality of life. This ultimate reality supports and nourishes humanity and all other living beings. Those who have perceived this ultimate reality inherent in their own lives truly know themselves; they are Buddhas.

cause and effect—Buddhism expounds the law of cause and effect that operates in life, ranging over past, present and future existences. This causality underlies the doctrine of karma. From this viewpoint, causes formed in the past are manifested as effects in the present. Causes formed in the present will be manifested as effects in the future. Buddhism emphasizes the causes one creates and accumulates in the present, because these will determine one's future. Nichiren taught that ordinary persons could manifest their innate Buddhahood (effect) through faith and practice, and then, based on Buddhahood, go out among the people of the nine worlds (cause) to lead them to Buddhahood.

Daisaku Ikeda—The third president of the Soka Gakkai and the current president of the Soka Gakkai International, is a Buddhist thinker, author and educator who believes that only through personal interaction and dialogue across cultural and philosophical boundaries can human beings nurture the trust and understanding that is necessary for lasting peace. To date, he has traveled to more than fifty countries in pursuit of this ideal, holding discussions with many distinguished political, cultural and educational figures. Topics include a range of issues crucial to humanity such as the transformative value of religion, the universality of life, social responsibility and sustainable progress and development.

In his view, global peace relies ultimately on a self-directed transformation within the life of the individual, rather than on societal or structural reforms alone. This idea is expressed most succinctly in his two novelized accounts of the Soka Gakkai's history, *The Human Revolution* and *the New Human Revolution*.

Ikeda is the founder of the Soka (value-creation) school system, which puts into practice the educational approach formulated by Tsunesaburo Makiguchi, first Soka Gakkai president, and Josei Toda. It is a nondenominational school system based on an ideal of fostering each student's unique creative potential and cultivating an ethic of peace, social contribution and global consciousness. The school system runs from kindergarten through graduate study and includes a university in Tokyo, Japan, and another in California, USA.

eternity of life—Buddhism's view of eternal life posits that one's life or essence has no real beginning or end. We live many lifetimes, repeating the cycle of birth and death. Like going to sleep at night, we refresh our bodies and wake up anew in circumstances that correspond to our karma (see karma). It is extremely fortunate to be born as a human being with the potential to improve our own life while contributing to the happiness of those around us.

Gohonzon—Nichiren Daishonin inscribed a mandala, the fundamental object of respect called the Gohonzon, on October 12, 1279. This object, in the form of a scroll, depicts, in Chinese characters, Nam-myoho-renge-kyo (the Law) and the life of Nichiren (the Person), as well as protective influences. Down the center of the Gohonzon are the characters *Nam-myoho-renge-kyo* and Nichiren's signature. This indicates the oneness of Person and Law—that the condition of Buddhahood is a potential within and can be manifested by all people. SGI members enshrine a replica of the original Gohonzon in their homes as a focal point for their daily practice. The Gohonzon's power comes from the practitioner's faith—the Gohonzon functions as a spiritual mirror. The actual Gohonzon exists within each person's life. Sitting in front of the Gohonzon and chanting, a person is able to recognize and reveal his or her own Buddha nature, the creative essence of life.

human revolution—Human revolution was a term used by Josei Toda, second president of the Soka Gakkai, to describe the process by which individuals gradually expand their lives, conquer their negative and destructive tendencies and ultimately make the state of Buddhahood their dominant life-condition. SGI President Daisaku Ikeda wrote the following words in the foreword to his novel *The Human Revolution,* "A great human revolution in just a single individual will help achieve a change in the destiny of a nation and further, will enable a change in the destiny of all humankind." It is with this spirit that members of the SGI pursue their own individual human revolution through their daily Buddhist practice and activities for world peace.

karma—Karma is the accumulation of effects from the good and bad causes that we bring with us from our former lives, as well as from the good and bad causes we have made in this lifetime, which shapes our future. Karma is a Sanskrit word that means action. Karma is created by actions—our thoughts, words and deeds—

and manifests itself in our appearance, behavior, attitudes, good and bad fortune and where we are born or live. In short—every-thing about us. It is all the positive and negative influences or causes that make up our complete reality in this world. This law of karmic causality operates in perpetuity, carrying over from one lifetime to the next and remaining with one in the latent state between death and rebirth.

Shakyamuni maintained that what makes a person noble or humble is not birth but one's actions. Therefore the Buddhist doctrine of karma is not fatalistic. Rather, karma is viewed not only as a means to explain the present, but also as the potential force through which to influence one's future. Buddhism therefore encourages people to create the best possible karma in the present in order to ensure the best possible outcome in the future.

Nichiren Buddhism does not consider one's karma or destiny to be fixed since our minds change from moment to moment, even the habitual and destructive tendencies we all possess to varying degrees can be altered. In other words, Buddhism teaches that individuals have within themselves the potential to change their own karma.

Lotus Sutra—This is the twenty-eight-chapter oral teaching, recorded in writing after the death of Shakyamuni, that benefited people during Shakyamuni's lifetime and during the Former Day of the Law. Whereas Shakyamuni expressed it as the "twenty-eight-chapter Lotus Sutra," Nichiren, to enable all human beings of the Latter Day to attain Buddhahood, revealed the ultimate principle of the Lotus Sutra as Nam-myoho-renge-kyo.

Since the Lotus Sutra was the central scriptural influence on Nichiren, it is worth mentioning one specific element in it that he thought was crucial. He taught that the Lotus Sutra proclaims that there is an inherent Buddha nature in all human beings. From this comes the idea that all people can attain Buddhahood as they are, as ordinary people in the phenomenal world. This rather revolutionary notion of the essential equality of men and women is central to Nichiren's understanding of the Lotus Sutra and was quite a radical thought at that time in history and in many places in the world even today.

Nam-myoho-renge-kyo—This is the ultimate Law or truth of the universe, according to Nichiren's teaching. Nichiren taught that the essence, all of the benefits of the wisdom contained, in the Lotus Sutra could be realized by chanting its title: [Nam]-myoho-renge-kyo. Chanting these words and excerpts from the Lotus Sutra is the core of this Buddhist practice, supported by study and the sharing of Buddhist teachings.

Nam (or Namu) derives from the Sanskrit word *namas* and is translated as devotion or as dedicating one's life. *Myo* stands for the Dharma nature, or enlightenment, while *ho* represents darkness or ignorance. Together as *myoho,* they express the idea that ignorance and the Dharma nature are a single entity or one in essence. *Renge* stands for the two elements of cause and effect. Cause and effect are also a single entity. *Kyo* represents the words and voices of all living beings. *Kyo* may also be defined as that which is constant and unchanging in the three existences of past, present and future.

Nichiren and Nichiren Buddhism—Nichiren (1222-1282) was the founder of the Buddhist tradition that is based on the Lotus Sutra and which urges chanting the phrase Nam-myoho-renge-kyo. Nichiren Buddhism was founded in 1253 in Japan. It is the Buddhism on which the activities of the SGI are based. It places special emphasis on the sanctity of human life and, as a natural outgrowth of this, on world peace. Lasting peace can only be realized by challenging and overcoming the inner impulse toward hatred and violence that exists within all people. Buddhism terms this inner impulse the "fundamental darkness of life." It is the dynamic process of self-reformation through the daily practice of Buddhism that results in the rejuvenation of the individual and society and forms the core of SGI's vision for a peaceful world.

nine consciousnesses. "Consciousness" is the translation of the Sanskrit *vijnana,* which means discernment.

The nine consciousnesses are:

(1) sight-consciousness

(2) hearing-consciousness

(3) smell-consciousness

(4) taste-consciousness

(5) touch-consciousness

(6) mind-consciousness

(7) *mano-consciousness*

(8) *alaya-consciousness*

(9) *amala-consciousness*

The first five consciousnesses correspond to the five senses of sight, hearing, smell, taste and touch. The sixth consciousness integrates the perceptions of the five senses into coherent images and makes judgments about the external world.

In contrast to the first six consciousnesses that deal with the external world, the seventh or *mano-consciousness* discerns the inner spiritual world. Awareness of and attachment to the self are said to originate from the *mano*-consciousness, as does the capacity to distinguish between good and evil. The eighth or *alaya-consciousness* is below the level of consciousness. It exists in what modern psychology calls the unconscious. All experiences of the present and previous lifetimes—collectively called karma—are stored there. It receives the *alaya-consciousness* thus forming the framework of individual existence.

The ninth consciousness, the *amala-con-sciousness,* lies below the *alaya-consciousness* and remains free from all karmic impurity. This ninth consciousness is defined as the basis of all spiritual functions and is identified with the true nature of life. It is the ninth consciousness that we effect when we chant Nam-myoho-renge-kyo.

oneness of life and its environment—This is also referred to as the non-duality of life and its environment. The principle of the oneness of life and its environment describes the inseparable relationship of the individual and the environment. People generally have a tendency to regard the environment as something separate from themselves, and from the viewpoint of that which we can physically observe, we are often justified in drawing this distinction. However, from the viewpoint of ultimate reality, the individual and the environment are one and inseparable. Life manifests itself in both a living subject and an objective environment.

Life indicates a subjective *self* that experiences the karmic effects of past actions. The environment is the objective realm where the karmic effects of life take shape. Environment here does not mean one overall context in which all beings live. Each living being has his or her unique environment in which the effects of karma appear. The effects of one's karma, both good and bad, manifest themselves both in one's self and in the environment, because these are two integral phases of the same entity.

Since both life and its environment are one, whichever of the Ten Worlds an individual manifests internally will be mirrored in his or her environment. Moreover, as people accumulate good karma through

Buddhist practice, the effects of that karma will become apparent not only in themselves but also in their environment, in the form of self-awareness, wisdom, improved circumstances, greater respect from others and so forth.

The principle of the oneness of life and its environment is the rationale for asserting that the Buddhist practice of individuals will work a transformation in society. Buddhism expands the entire reality of life and shows the way to live a winning life—the most fulfilled existence.

Shakyamuni (Siddhartha Gautama)—Buddhism arose in what is now India about 500 bce out of the teachings of Shakyamuni, Siddhartha Gautama, also known as the Buddha, "the Enlightened One." Tradition has it that although Gautama's father kept him in princely isolation during his youth, brief glimpses of the pain experienced by ordinary people led him to one of his most fundamental realizations: Life is predicated on suffering and change. This general truth of suffering is emblematically represented in Buddhism as the four sufferings of birth, aging, sickness and death. Confronted with the dilemma of such universal suffering, Shakyamuni, at an early age, decided to renounce his claim to his father's throne and embark on a search for the way to alleviate the pain embodied in these four. After several years of the most extreme form of asceticism, finding himself no closer to an answer, he concluded that the path to understanding that he sought lay neither in asceticism nor in the luxurious life of his youth, but in between them, in a "middle way." Abandoning his ascetic practice and meditating deeply through the night, he destroyed his remaining impurities, eliminated his false views and experienced the goal of Buddhahood.

Thus began the career of one of the great religious figures of history. By all accounts he was a man of boundless compassion and peace. By the time of his death, thousands had been converted to the new wisdom he propounded. Some of those converts joined his monastic order, renouncing the secular world; many did not. After his death, his many teachings were compiled into the twenty-eight-chapter Lotus Sutra.

Soka Gakkai International (SGI)—The Soka Gakkai or Value-Creating Society, is a Buddhist lay organization founded in Japan on November 18, 1930, by Tsunesaburo Makiguchi, who became its first president, and his disciple, Josei Toda. Makiguchi regarded the creation of values that are conducive to a happy life as the purpose of education. In 1928 he encountered the teachings of Nichiren and the Lotus Sutra and found in them resonance with his philosophy of value.

Later, Makiguchi and Toda were arrested for opposing the policies of the Japanese militarist regime and

imprisoned as a thought criminal. Makiguchi died in prison at the age of 73 and Toda, upon his release, revived the organization after World War II, building it, as its second president, into a dynamic, popular movement with 750,000 members in Japan.

Daisaku Ikeda became the third president of the Soka Gakkai in 1960 and is now the president of the Soka Gakkai International which has spread to more than 190 countries and territories with more than twelve million members.

The SGI aims to realize the absolute happiness (enlightenment) of individuals and the prosperity of each country by spreading understanding of the Buddhism of Nichiren Daishonin. Toward that end, the SGI engages in various activities to promote peace, culture and education.

The SGI's membership reflects a broad range of ethnic and social diversity. In the United States, the SGI-USA (www.sgi-usa.org) has over 100 community centers throughout the country. Discussion meetings are conducted monthly in private homes where practicing members and friends study the philosophy, share experiences and have heart-to-heart dialogue.

Printed in Great Britain
by Amazon